EXONERATED

THE FAILED TAKEDOWN
OF PRESIDENT DONALD TRUMP
BY THE SWAMP

Also by Dan Bongino

Spygate: The Attempted Sabotage of Donald J. Trump

EXONERATED

THE FAILED TAKEDOWN
OF PRESIDENT DONALD TRUMP
BY THE SWAMP

DAN BONGINO

Post Hill
PRESS

A POST HILL PRESS BOOK

Exonerated:
The Failed Takedown of President Donald Trump by the Swamp
© 2019 by Dan Bongino
All Rights Reserved

ISBN: 978-1-64293-341-3
ISBN (eBook): 978-1-64293-342-0

Cover design by Cody Corcoran

Post Hill Press
New York • Nashville
posthillpress.com

Published in the United States of America

*A heartfelt thank-you to all of the citizen journalists
who filled in the massive holes left behind by the alleged journalists
who failed to cover the most significant political spying scandal
of our time. You did the job our broken media failed to do.
Special thanks to 279.*

CONTENTS

INTRODUCTION

At its beginning, Russiagate was a plug-and-play operation. Then it picked up steam and spun out of control as investigators searched in vain for connections that never existed. But at the start, it relied on a template for manufacturing a national scandal. The template wasn't a formal diagram; it was more conceptual—a plan based on two newspaper articles that had been hiding in plain sight. Taken together, however, these stories provided a dangerous playbook for an attempt to take down Donald Trump.

All this lethal political formula needed to be activated was the right mix, the perfect plug-and-play components to detonate conspiracy charges: take a toxic, compromised political operative and tie him to a nationally known figure running for president, then connect the candidate to a few nasty rumors from murky sources, and presto! You've just created the pretext for a devastating scandal—complete with an explosion of muck for the media to rake over the front-running candidate while also providing the ammunition to fuel partisan politicians' demands for an investigation.

This book exposes that template and the people who used it to ignite the deep state attack on Donald Trump. It reverse-engineers the entire sordid, disgraceful operation that was meant, initially, to discredit the Trump campaign and stop him from becoming president.

Prepare to be outraged. Explosive revelations are going to come at a fast and furious pace. *Exonerated* exposes the following:

How a profiteering ex-journalist stumbled on the connections of one shady lobbyist—a now convicted tax evader who is serving seven-and-a-half years in the United States Penitentiary, Canaan, near Scranton, Pennsylvania—to cast a shadow over an entire election campaign.

How the ex-scribe armed with a contract to conduct opposition research to find damning information about Donald Trump in the run-up to the 2016 presidential campaign hired a Russia expert—who just happened to be married to a senior Justice Department official—and then later lobbied her spouse to open an investigation on the front-running candidate, Donald Trump.

How the template mastermind then hired former British intelligence officer Christopher Steele, who was viewed favorably by the FBI, and fed him information, turning him into some out-of-control quote machine. Steele eventually helped launder these sleazy "findings" into semiofficial-sounding allegations.

How those allegations—in the form of the infamous "Steele dossier"—were fed to politicians and journalists, and how Steele doubledipped, joining the FBI payroll and feeding similar reports to the FBI to legitimize these fictions and to force an official probe.

How some of the top law enforcement and intelligence agents in the nation—men and women shocked by the rise of a maverick candidate and horrified by the idea that Hillary Clinton might lose the election to a swamp outsider—worked to create an aura of conspiracy around Donald Trump and his campaign and then to cripple his presidency.

How, after being spoon-fed dubious allegations by the former journalist, senior FBI leaders skirted official investigation protocols to initiate investigations—which then served to legitimize the flimsy and often completely bogus evidence.

How the FBI leaders, using these bogus allegations and a previous investigation of a low-profile Trump advisor, then went to America's secret, rubber-stamp warrant factory to obtain permission to scrutinize this "evidence" and the entire Trump campaign.

How those warrants were then used to investigate—a polite term for "spy on"—American citizens tied to Trump and the campaign.

How, in the paranoid rush to find damning evidence that never existed in the first place, these lawmen also investigated family and friends of the campaign workers.

How these lawmen played extreme hardball with Trump team members, and how, after uncovering wrongdoings that had nothing to do with Russiagate, they tried to leverage potential criminal charges in an effort to substantiate collusion allegations—and repeatedly failed.

I have discussed many aspects of these mind-numbing deep state maneuvers on my podcasts. But the scope is so enormous that it takes a book to lay out the details in sequence—and sometimes in parallel—to document the cause-and-effect chaos that ensued.

"Conspiracy" and "collusion" are words that get thrown around a lot. From the earliest days of Russiagate, the two "C-words" have been everywhere. The FBI, the media, and deep state actors love those terms when they are related to Trump, Russian president Vladimir Putin, and the election. But one crippling fact remains: there has been no hard evidence of actual wrongdoing regarding the Trump campaign in connection with Russia, and after three solid years of warrants, wiretaps, threatening interviews, sensational arrests, countless leaks, and millions of dollars spent, special counsel Robert Mueller's supposed dream team of investigators has found *no evidence* of a nefarious collusion plot.

It turns out that, if anything, those highly charged C-words—"conspiracy" and "collusion"—should be applied to the investigators and the investigation itself. And we will get to that.

But let me be clear: I don't think there was a single figure orchestrating all of the events that I document here. Every player had a part to play, and the motivations of the all the players vary, but there was no grand puppet master. There was no Godfather. And there was no secret society, either. There were plenty of bad actors, no doubt—deep state figures with extensive ties to Hillary Clinton and Barack Obama—but keeping secrets wasn't their strong suit. The spinning of Russiagate was reactive, situational, and adversarial—no question. And for some of the bad actors, it was cynical, too. That goes double for the man behind the plug-and-play template. His plan, the plug-and-play ploy to discredit Trump, succeeded in hoodwinking top lawmen—although as we will see, some of those high-ranking law-and-order men had reasons to want to be deceived.

But this was no formal cabal. It was more, as I said, reactive—like an investigatory domino theory. In a series of colossal screw-ups that recall the Keystone Kops more than the Avengers, lawmen got conned and then had to join the con or risk being exposed and humiliated. In the end, faced with a lack of evidence and huge political expectations generated by leaks and an almost pathological hatred of Trump, the investigators were forced to cover their collective asses and generate more warrants and more arrests without ever getting close to proving a collusion conspiracy—because there never was one.

This resulted is a sequence of three seat-of-the-pants strategies that I call Plan A, Plan B, and Plan C. These were investigative tactics to spy on and probe Donald Trump and his campaign. When Plan A blew up, lawmen needed another course of action to cover for the faulty logic and flimsy evidence that launched the probe in the first place.

Usually, investigations spur cover-ups. But in this case, the opposite seems to have happened. Plans A, B, and C were cover-ups that served to legitimize the investigation!

Look, unwinding the plot to entrap Donald Trump is complicated—especially with my talking in general terms. The central players have more connections than the New York subway system. And there were all kinds of double-talk and suspect allegiances. So unpacking it all means tying everything together and moving back and forth in time. But stick with it and all will become clear. Warning: the truth may leave you aghast and horrified. I speak from experience. I've been sorting through the muck for three years and I'm still in shock.

I want to start with the template itself, the plug-and-play model that made Russiagate snowball. Then I want to introduce the cast of characters—or should I say perpetrators?—and their vested interests in the investigation and with one another. Then it will be time to unspool Plans A, B, and C and explain how they imploded.

America has suffered a national scandal. But it is not the one the nation was initially sold. The facts I unfurl reveal shocking truths. Put them together and you have a picture of a much different debacle, one that has destabilized our government and ripped apart our nation.

And it's really a tragedy. We are all suffering. This country has real problems to solve—the economy, health care, the opioid crisis, and much more. A bogus, politicized crisis is the last thing anyone needs.

America needs to manufacture jobs, not scandals. I hope exposing this plug-and-play template will prevent political hits in the future. Of course, it may do just the opposite, given all the political opportunists out there. But I have to share what I know. The story of *Exonerated* needs to be told.

Here it goes.

CHAPTER 1

The Plug-and-Play Plan

On April 17, 2007, the *Wall Street Journal* ran an article with the headline "How Lobbyists Help Ex-Soviets Woo Washington." On the surface, the piece was based on the oldest story in Washington, D.C.—that money buys influence and favors.

I know. You're thinking, "Stop the presses!"

But back in 2007, the most significant news angle of the piece was whom, exactly, appeared to be bought and who the buyers were.

One bombshell charge involving one household name drove the story: "For a $560,000 fee, Bob Dole, the former Senate majority leader and 1996 Republican presidential nominee, helped a Russian billionaire accused by rivals of bribery obtain a visa to visit the U.S. in 2005, among other things."[1]

As scandals go, you could file the revelations of this story under Typical Washington Cesspool Behavior. There was nothing, from Dole's point of view, illegal about it. It was part and parcel of what his law firm, along with so many others, did: open doors for clients. True, Dole's pulling favors for a billionaire Russian with reputed ties to the criminal underworld looked pretty sleazy. But otherwise, it was just another story about money and influence running amok in the capital. Sadly, this is old news.

For the purposes of Russiagate and the future tarnishing of Donald Trump's campaign, however, this article was filled with names of far more interest than Bob Dole's.

The billionaire that Dole and his law firm went to bat for was Oleg Deripaska, one of the world's richest men and reportedly one of Vladimir Putin's closest oligarch pals. Words and phrases like "illegal wiretapping," "extortion," and "racketeering" also follow his name with alarming frequency. Concerns about Deripaska's ties to criminal elements and antidemocratic regimes are generally thought to have caused his ongoing visa difficulties with the State Department.[2]

The article's more shocking revelation, though, was the implication that Dole and Deripaska were put in contact by Dole's old campaign advisor, a guy who also had made millions working for a veritable who's who of despotic leaders, including the infamous former Ukrainian president Viktor Yanukovych.

A guy named, as you probably guessed, Paul Manafort.

We'll get to why Manafort's presence in the article is so important—and why he was such a liability to Donald Trump. But first, let's finish with the other notable name in the *Journal* story. It's arguably the most shocking name of all, and it's right there below the headline: Glenn Simpson, who cowrote the story with his wife, Mary Jacoby.[3]

More than any other figure in Donald Trump's orbit, Paul Manafort deserved to set off alarm bells when it came to Russia. But more than any other figure in the entire Russiagate charade, Glenn Simpson is the one who actually pulled the alarms.

Simpson knew just how explosive Manafort's presence in the campaign was, in part because of this article.

As many readers may know, Simpson no longer works as an investigative reporter for the *Journal*. Instead, he runs Fusion GPS, the strategic intelligence firm hired in late 2015 by the *Washington Free*

Beacon to conduct opposition research on Donald Trump. The *Beacon*, a conservative media outlet, claims it also paid for research on other Republican candidates.[4] In late 2015, Simpson approached Nellie Ohr, a Russia specialist who is married to Associate Deputy Attorney General Bruce Ohr, one of the highest-ranking officials in the Department of Justice (DOJ). Simpson hired Nellie, eventually paying her $44,000, and he would later lobby Bruce[5]—acts that would subsequently derail the DOJ bigwig's career.

But then, in the spring of 2016, Simpson got lucky.

Extremely lucky.

The big misstep of the Trump campaign—probably the one appointment those involved would like to take back—occurred.

On March 29, 2016, Paul Manafort was named campaign convention manager. At the time, Fusion GPS's work on anti-Trump research for the *Beacon* had come to an end. But with Manafort now part of the Trump team, a whole new river of muck presented itself to Simpson. And when six weeks later, on April 16, 2016, Manafort became Donald Trump's campaign manager, Simpson must have pulled the article out of his back pocket and danced a jig. If anyone wanted opposition research, he had the golden ticket—the golden template—right in front of him, in the article he had written precisely nine years and one day earlier.

That same spring, Simpson and Fusion GPS were able to reportedly wrangle more than $1 million from Perkins Coie, the law firm representing the Democratic National Committee and the Clinton campaign, to continue his anti-Trump research.[6]

And part of that research, no doubt, involved one specific sentence in that old, yellowing article. It was a sentence that, incredibly, suggested that Manafort had committed a crime—one that would haunt not only Manafort but at least two other members of the Trump team: "Mr. Manafort, who isn't registered as a consultant to the Ukrainian leader, didn't respond to requests for comment."[7]

With that one sentence, Simpson and Jacoby quietly set up Manafort and anyone he would work with in the future. They were blowing a whistle for federal investigators, suggesting in black and white that Paul Manafort had violated the Foreign Agents Registration Act (FARA), a law requiring agents and lobbyists representing the interests of foreign powers in a "political or quasi-political capacity" to register with the Department of Justice.

So opposition researcher Glenn Simpson—the man hired to provide actionable intelligence to cripple Donald Trump's campaign—had figured out years earlier that Manafort might be vulnerable to criminal charges. Now he could plug that fact into his case against Trump.

Flush with money from the DNC and Clinton, Simpson hired Christopher Steele, the former head of MI6's Russia desk, to compile intelligence briefings on possible Russian influencing operations regarding the 2016 presidential election. This was Simpson's key hire. He paid Steele's firm, Orbis Business Intelligence, $168,000.[8] In return, he got the former intelligence operative who had also worked for and with the FBI. He was a known, respected entity who could feed "information" to intelligence and investigative channels and who could pass on the information that Simpson amassed.

Or, perhaps, created.

That information is now known as the "Steele dossier." It contains an avalanche of misinformation and lies about Donald Trump, his associates, and alleged Russian influencing. But when it was leaked—first to liberal *Mother Jones* editor David Corn and later to *BuzzFeed*, which published the entire thing, as well as a number of political and intelligence figures—it drove the outcry of C-word allegations and helped spur Russiagate investigations.

Simpson's wife, Mary Jacoby, was so proud of her husband that she later outed him as masterminding these fantasy filings—wanting to make sure that he got credit for the work instead of Steele. "It's come to my attention that some people still don't realize what Glenn's role was in exposing Putin's control of Donald Trump," Jacoby wrote in a June 24, 2017, Facebook post, according to online magazine *Tablet*. "Let's be clear. Glenn conducted the investigation. Glenn hired Chris Steele. Chris Steele worked for Glenn."[9]

This is one of the most damning quotes in the entire Russiagate affair and we will return to it soon, when we discuss the dossier in greater detail. But for now, just keep it in the back of your mind as evidence of Simpson's scandal-fabricating activity.

Let's go back to Simpson's 2007 *Wall Street Journal* article for a brief moment—and its importance in engulfing the Trump campaign in a cyclone of dubious charges.

Simpson's story suggests that Manafort, among other things, may have committed a FARA violation. True, FARA crimes are rarely, if ever, enforced in lobbyist-loving Washington. But evidence of criminal behavior is exactly what investigators needed to open a probe. With Manafort's proximity to Trump—and Manafort's well-documented connections to Putin's pal Viktor Yanukovych, the scandal-ridden, corrupt former president of Ukraine who bolted to Russia after being overthrown—Simpson had almost everything he needed to start a firestorm.

I say "almost" because there was one other old story that shaped the template by tying Manafort to another prominent political leader who (like Dole) had run for president: John McCain. When it comes to providing further instructions for how to weaponize the Trump campaign against itself, this article was even more powerful.

The article, "Aide Helped Controversial Russian Meet McCain," by Jeffrey H. Birnbaum and John Solomon, appeared in the Friday, January 25, 2008, issue of the *Washington Post*. It focuses on the disturbing connections between McCain's 2008 presidential campaign manager, Rick Davis, and Oleg Deripaska. Davis, of course, was part of Davis Manafort Inc., which the paper describes as "a lobbying firm that was being paid to provide political advice to pro-Russian and oligarch-funded candidates in Ukraine."[10]

The presence of Davis, who attended and evidently facilitated two meetings between McCain and Deripaska in 2006, caused a good deal of friction within the McCain campaign team, the article reveals. Some aides believed that Davis's firm's work overseas conflicted with the senator's record as a pro-democracy champion and an advocate of reducing the influence of lobbyists in Washington. Because of this, "the aides questioned whether Davis should be given an important title in the campaign because that would make him more vulnerable to criticism," sources told the reporters.[11]

Campaign aides weren't the only ones worried about Davis's presence or McCain's potentially problematic ties to Davis-Manafort. John Weaver, one of McCain's top advisors in the 2008 campaign, says U.S. intelligence raised concerns to McCain's staff about the Davis-Manafort work. (It might have been helpful if those same agents had tipped off Trump to Manafort's problematic past, but interestingly, that courtesy call never happened.)

According to Sara A. Carter, writing in the now defunct news site *Circa*, a U.S. counterintelligence source confirmed the concern about a possible McCain influencing operation. "Before there was Trump, there were concerns about some of the same people being around McCain about ten years ago, and we alerted his team to those concerns and they appeared to take some defensive action."[12]

Manafort remains offstage for most of the *Washington Post* article—although it reports that Deripaska thanked him in a letter for helping arrange the meeting with McCain in Davos, Switzerland—but it's clear that his proximity to Davis and Deripaska tainted him tangentially.

So here we come back to the plug-and-play scandal operation. Anti-Trump operatives saw a clear opportunity: if they substituted the names Trump and Manafort for McCain and Davis, they could recycle the previous scandal that had plagued McCain in 2008. Because of Manafort's dirty past, they could taint the Trump campaign with the same bad optics, the same public relations nightmares, the same potential conflicts of interest and, most damning of all, the same concerns about Russian influencing. In fact, Manafort's Russian connections would be even more inflammatory when tied to Trump because the candidate had made statements on the stump about wanting to work more closely with Russia and had given speeches listing some of the interests that Moscow and D.C. shared. In the toxic shadow of Manafort, those comments became more troubling. Trump's campaign manager was connected to some of the most repressive and sinister Russian figures. He took their money. These facts don't actually prove that Trump did anything wrong (he didn't), but they provided opposition operatives everything they needed to scream collusion and push for an investigation.

So the main components for a plug-and-play plan were now, finally, in place, ready to be activated to detonate a scandal of epic proportions.

But Simpson wasn't the only one in town with his eye on Manafort. A longtime consultant for the Democratic National Committee named Alexandra Chalupa had been waiting for him to appear, too.

"I felt there was a Russia connection," Chalupa told *Politico*. "And that, if there was, that we can expect Paul Manafort to be involved in this election." For Chalupa, whose Democratic bona fides also include working at the White House's Office of Public Liaison for the Clinton administration, Manafort was "Putin's political brain for manipulating U.S. foreign policy and elections."[13]

Chalupa shifted into overdrive once Manafort joined Trump. A week after Manafort officially signed on to Team Trump, she met with a legislative assistant in the office of Representative Marcy Kaptur, Democrat of Ohio, as well as cochairs of the Congressional Ukrainian Caucus, and pushed for a congressional investigation. An email Chalupa sent to the DNC communications director[14] at the beginning of May that was subsequently hacked and eventually published by WikiLeaks reveals that she claimed to have been working "for the past few weeks" with Yahoo! News star reporter Michael Isikoff.[15] That would appear to tie her to Isikoff's April 26, 2016, story, "Trump's campaign chief is questioned about ties to Russian billionaire," which reveals that Manafort had been questioned by officials from the Cayman Islands "in connection with a $26.2 million investment by a billionaire Russian oligarch who was his partner in an ill-fated telecommunications development in Ukraine."[16]

Chalupa left the DNC—which had paid her $412,000 from 2004 to June 2016, according to Federal Election Commission records—after the Democratic convention in late July to focus full-time on her research on Manafort, Trump, and Russia.

She was not alone. Simpson and Steele were assembling the dossier, of course. And the Never Trumpers were gaining momentum. They had real motivation now. Trump had officially become the Republican nominee on June 16. That meant he was the only one standing in the way of Hillary Clinton in her mission to take control of the White House. The deep state was on high alert. Meanwhile, Vladimir Putin must have been exceedingly pleased. A declassified national security assessment determined that Putin had "ordered an influence campaign" targeting the U.S. election.[17]

Putin, angered by U.S. sanctions and his nation's own diminished stature, ordered all three Russia intelligence agencies—the Federal Security Service (FSB), the Foreign Intelligence Service (SVR), and the Main Intelligence Directorate (GRU)—to wreak havoc. While Putin had plenty of reasons to hate Hillary Clinton, and while cyberagents working for Russian intelligence were clearly targeting the DNC—eventually hacking, stealing, and releasing a trove of emails on WikiLeaks—the idea that Russia has any allegiance to the Republican party is ludicrous. Ronald Reagan, the Republican Party's figurehead, destroyed the Soviet Union with covert operations in the 1980s that wrecked its economy. Putin, serving as a KGB big shot, witnessed the national humiliation of his beloved Mother Russia at the hands of the U.S. So rest assured that all he has ever wanted to do is sow discord in the United States and destabilize our nation. He knew he couldn't actually afford to go to war against us, so this was the next best thing: foment distrust and conspiracy theories and destroy America from within.

If anyone has any doubts about this, one of Putin's closest advisors, Vladislav Surkov, actually spelled out Moscow's savage goals in an article published in February 2019, saying, "Foreign politicians talk about Russia's interference in elections and referendums around the world. In fact, the matter is even more serious: Russia interferes in your brains, we change your conscience, and there is nothing you can do about it."[18]

Putin, in other words, wanted us to eat ourselves alive.

Unfortunately, a veritable army of Washington insiders was making it easy for him.

CHAPTER 2

The Cast: Conflicts 'R' Us

It's time to unwind how we went from a Glenn Simpson article in the *Wall Street Journal* to a multimillion-dollar special counsel probe that divided the nation, partially paralyzed the Trump administration, and accomplished little more than to make dozens of lawyers richer than they were two years prior. So let's focus on the key players who drove this colossal fiasco. Many of them are former colleagues. Some have tight relationships with opposition leaders like Barack Obama and Hillary Clinton. Some have ugly legal skeletons in their closet. And some are career lawmen who bought into shrewd opposition research that was calculated to look much more damaging than it was.

Getting spun in public on the biggest story in decades is not fun. Getting fed bogus evidence and then biting it is humiliating and embarrassing. It can make you look bad. Actually, when you get played in public and wind up powering a gargantuan probe that draws Watergate comparisons—an investigation fabricated to cast doubt on the legitimacy of a presidential election—that isn't just bad; it's catastrophic.

Seriously, it doesn't just ruin your search results online. It can kill your entire career.

This is what seems to have driven many of the principal characters here. They bought a sham story and then had to engage in face-saving maneuvers later after the stunning upset that was the electoral victory of Donald Trump. Forced to adjust on the fly—when blockbuster allegations began to disintegrate—these ace investigators and attorneys widened the scope of the probe—a kind of legal plug-and-play, if you will—to increase the chance of finding wrongdoing somewhere.

The result? Russiagate has turned up zero collusion-related charges alleged in Glenn Simpson and Christopher Steele's dossier. Again, there have been no collusion charges in any way, shape, or form. Any arrests and indictments from the special counsel investigation—of former Trump administration National Security Advisor Michael Flynn, former campaign official Paul Manafort, and former campaign advisor George Papadopoulos—have nothing to do with the president or the Trump campaign. Say what you want about them, but they didn't collude with Russians.

Looking at this cast of characters and defining their motives—why they've done what they've done and their self-serving special interests in the investigation—is critical to understanding how Russiagate spiraled out of control despite the fact that *nobody* on the campaign colluded with the Russians, which was the stated reason for the special counsel investigation.

JOHN BRENNAN

The poster boy for Never Trumpers, CIA director John Brennan has been a cheerleader for Russiagate from the beginning. A twenty-five-year intelligence community veteran, he is widely regarded as an overly ambitious political climber and a swamp creature who backed Hillary Clinton and was anxious to serve as her CIA chief, as he had for Barack Obama.

His unhinged venom toward Donald Trump reached a fever pitch with an acidic tweet after the president's Helsinki press conference. Trump's performance "rises & exceeds the threshold of 'high crimes & misdemeanors,'" Brennan ranted. "It was nothing short of treasonous. Not only were Trump's comments imbecilic, he is wholly in the pocket of Putin."[1]

Normally, charges like that coming from America's former spymaster would be devastating. If anyone was in a position to know about damning proof of collusion and collaboration, it would be the former CIA chief, right?

But the Mueller report now stands as proof that it was Brennan, not Trump, who was off his rocker. But why?

The reason lies in the genesis of Russiagate. When Trump, the ultimate outsider candidate, began mentioning Russia in his stump speeches and said a few positive things about our former Cold War enemy, it shocked the establishment. A presidential candidate was seeking a better relationship with Russia? It was inconceivable to the know-it-all foreign policy pundits who resented any contrarian views from outside of their elitist bubbles. Establishment cold warriors in D.C. would have none of it. But there was nothing these naysayers could do, really. This is America, where freedom of speech is a fundamental right, and you can't just wiretap an American citizen for openly considering working with a foreign country.

But if you run the CIA, you have powerful international connections who can. Which is to say, while American intelligence can't spy on its own citizens in most cases, its foreign colleagues—with their less restrictive surveillance laws—can.

That's what spies do. They spy. As Lee Smith reports in *Tablet*, certain circles in Washington had been awash in rumors that "Britain's intelligence service, the Government Communications Headquarters, was intercepting the emails and phone calls of Trump officials."[2]

Brennan's overseas intelligence connections began relaying back information about "figures connected to Trump and known or suspected Russian agents" as early as 2015, according to the *Guardian*.[3] And BBC reports that Brennan was told in April 2016 about an alleged tape recording that mentioned Kremlin cash "going into the US presidential campaign."[4]

In August 2016, Brennan told then Senate majority leader Harry Reid that Russians were interfering in our election on Trump's behalf, relaying the same information originating from Steele and Simpson. Brennan's brief pushed Reid to write a letter to then FBI director James Comey citing "evidence of a direct connection" between the Trump campaign, and he urged an investigation.[5]

Eventually, the pressure worked. This intel, along with the Steele dossier, was used to obtain a Foreign Intelligence Surveillance Act (FISA) warrant to spy on Donald Trump and Trump campaign figures.

So Brennan was invested in seeing this intelligence—much of which he seems to have processed into his tweets—proven out. He was instrumental in getting the Russiagate probe off the ground. And he wanted to be proven right.

It's also worth noting that under Brennan, the CIA did conduct spy operations on selected Americans and was never penalized for repeated violations.[6] He experienced almost no political fallout, which is to say that Brennan himself knows something about high crimes and misdemeanors—or at least getting away with them.

JAMES CLAPPER

James Clapper, director of national intelligence from 2010 to 2017, was a spymaster who was heavily invested in ensuring Donald Trump's defeat and also had plenty of skin in the game. Since leaving his job, Clapper has consistently painted Trump as a possible Russian asset, and he was instrumental in helping legitimize Simpson and Steele's information and dossier.[7] He also had a very good reason for doing so: Clapper had plenty to lose in the event of an ideological regime change. He is a known liar with regard to intrusive U.S. government surveillance.

On March 12, 2013, Clapper testified in an open congressional hearing. Senator Ron Wyden, Democrat of Oregon, asked the intel chief who heads the sixteen intelligence-gathering operations of the federal government: "Does the NSA collect any type of data at all on millions, or hundreds of millions, of Americans?"

"No, sir," Clapper replied. "Not wittingly."

It was a bald-faced lie.[8]

A mere three months later, Edward Snowden leaked his treasure trove of classified National Security Administration (NSA) documents revealing that the agency had been vacuuming up data on domestic and international communications, exposing Clapper's falsehood.

Lying to Congress under oath is against the law and can get you up to five years in prison.

Clapper later issued a bizarre defense, insisting that Wyden's simple yes-or-no question was some mind-bogglingly complex query. In fact, he compared it to being asked a "When are you going to stop beating your wife?" kind of question—the kind of inquiry that implies something unproven is a fact. Then he said the query was "not answerable necessarily, by a simple yes or no. So I responded in what I thought was the most truthful or least untruthful manner, by saying, 'No.'"[9]

It's hard not to think about Clapper's legacy, though, when you consider his dishonest record on intrusive spying and what he did to get the Steele dossier into the national press and to push Russiagate into the mainstream. Clapper advised FBI director James Comey to brief then president-elect Trump on the Steele dossier. On Friday, January 6, 2017, Comey met with Trump and his transition team at Trump Tower and shared some of the allegations. Four days later, on January 10, CNN, *BuzzFeed*, and other outlets revealed that the meeting had taken place and that the president had learned of the charges contained in the dossier—which instantly bestowed a sense of legitimacy on the now debunked and entirely unsubstantiated report. The very next day, January 11, Clapper issued a statement claiming he conveyed his own shock and outrage about the leaks to the incoming president, saying, "I expressed my profound dismay at the leaks that have been appearing in the press."

Evidence suggests that Clapper may have been lying then, too. In April 2018, Republicans on the House Intelligence Committee released a report on the run-up to Russiagate. "Clapper subsequently acknowledged discussing the 'dossier with CNN journalist Jake Tapper,' and admitted that he might have spoken with other journalists about the same topic," the report asserts[10]—a charge Clapper later denied in a TV interview.

Months later, Clapper got a new job. Leaking to CNN seems to have been a profitable move; the network subsequently hired him as a contributor. He personally profited by helping promote the Russiagate hoax and by damaging Donald Trump.

Meanwhile, he has also started off-loading any responsibility for the Russiagate investigation—passing it off on Barack Obama, as seen in an interview with Anderson Cooper:

> *If it weren't for President Obama, we might not have done the intelligence community assessment that we did that set off a whole sequence of events which are still unfolding today, notably, special counsel Mueller's investigation. President Obama is responsible for that, and it was he who tasked us to do that intelligence community assessment in the first place.*[11]

PAUL MANAFORT

I've already made it clear that Manafort is a troubled actor in Russiagate. That said, given what happened to others in the campaign, deep state operatives would have targeted "suspects" to justify the bogus scandal—like George Papadopoulos, who made no secret about trying to arrange a meeting with Moscow on behalf of the campaign. But let's face it: Manafort was the Achilles heel of the whole campaign.

Given everything that's come to light about him over the past three years, it's easy to say that there were warning signs in Manafort's previous work. That implies that the Trump campaign should have realized he was a liability. But that is an unduly harsh assessment. Remember, Trump was an outsider and Manafort, given his long lobbying résumé, must have painted himself as the ultimate insider. Not only that, but Manafort even had a model of his own to follow provided by Rick Davis, his old partner at Manafort Davis Inc., who had talked his way into becoming John McCain's campaign chair in 2008.

Manafort, it turns out, had numerous motives for joining Team Trump. As a longtime Republican consultant, he brought valuable experience, insight, and connections to the campaign. But he also had a ten-million-dollar debt to Oleg Deripaska that was hanging over his head, according to tax return records.[12] That is a hefty, potentially compromising debt, especially if Deripaska's reputation for engaging in mob-like solutions isn't just a rumor. This link alone would have made him damaged goods. But as we've seen, he had a boatload of debt, tax, and legal issues on top of the violations Glenn Simpson had already written about.

GLENN SIMPSON

Here are the known facts about Glenn Simpson. As a reporter for the *Wall Street Journal*, he wrote the previously mentioned 2007 article about Russian oligarchs influencing Washington that indicated he suspected Paul Manafort had violated FARA laws. He left the *Wall Street Journal* to start Fusion GPS. He was hired to conduct opposition research on Donald Trump. He hired Nellie Ohr, the wife of the fourth-highest-ranking DOJ official, Bruce Ohr, to conduct opposition research on Trump.

On October 16, 2018, Simpson invoked the Fifth Amendment—the right not to incriminate himself—when he was called to testify before a joint committee of Congress. A number of political insiders have speculated that Simpson may have perjured himself with previous testimony claiming he didn't meet Ohr until after the election.[13] As Representative John Ratcliffe, Republican of Texas, told Fox News' Maria Bartiromo in October 2018:

> Simpson had previously testified under oath to the House Intelligence Committee that he never met with Bruce Ohr or discussed with Bruce Ohr the Steele dossier prior to the October FISA application in 2016 or the 2016 presidential election. That is in direct contradiction to what Bruce Ohr told me under oath last month.[14]

Circumstantial evidence also suggests Simpson was neck-deep in the infamous Trump Tower meeting on June 9, 2016—despite his repeated denials. This meeting was initially portrayed as the smoking gun for the collusion charges between the Trump campaign and Russia. But overwhelming evidence suggests it was an entrapment scheme designed to gather negative political opposition research on the Trump campaign—not a juicy political dirt-swap.

The meeting was set in motion when British music promoter Rob Goldstone emailed Donald Trump Jr., promising the Russian "crown prosecutor" had information that would "incriminate Hillary and her dealings with Russia." Goldstone's client Emin Agalarov, the pop star son of Azerbaijani-Russian billionaire Aras Agalarov, also helped with the arrangements.

When reports of Goldstone's email—which looked damning—and the meeting surfaced in July 2017, the irresponsible, Trump-hating media had a field day.

But that email come-on proved to be a bait-and-switch ploy. The meeting was attended by Trump Jr., Paul Manafort, Jared Kushner, Natalia Veselnitskaya (a lawyer for the Russian holding company

Prevezon), lobbyist Rinat Akhmetshin, and two others. Veselnitskaya's primary mission was to advocate for overturning the Magnitsky Act, a congressional act that resulted in, among other things, the seizure of $230 million of Prevezon funds.

Veselnitskaya produced a memo that suggested the American firm Ziff Brothers Investments, which she claimed had helped Magnitsky Act advocate Bill Browder illegally buy up Gazprom shares, had "financed the Hillary Clinton campaign." As bombshells go, this was a disappointment, as similar claims had surfaced previously.

But here's the fascinating catch: the strategist who worked with Veselnitskaya to dig up dirt on Browder was the same strategist who had set the Steele dossier in motion—Glenn Simpson.

Members of what I call the Collusion Chorus like to point out that after the meeting leaked and the *New York Times* reported that Donald Trump Jr. was "promised damaging information about Hillary Clinton before agreeing to meet with a Kremlin-connected Russian lawyer during the 2016 campaign," the president actually dictated a statement to the press about the substance of the gathering. This presidential misstep was made under duress; Trump was reacting to unfounded and, as we will see, poisonous allegations and a cloud of "gotcha" media suspicion. But he later wisely faced down the fire with facts, tweeting, "This was a meeting to get information on an opponent, totally legal and done all the time in politics—and it went nowhere. I did not know about it!"

Glenn Simpson also claimed not to know about the meeting—despite admitting he met with his client Veselnitskaya hours before she visited Trump Tower and the following day. This of course, defies credulity. But Simpson insisted before a Senate committee that his client had a meeting with the son of the presumptive Republican presidential nominee, but somehow the meeting never came up.

Yeah, right.

Then there are the things about Simpson that I like to call the known unknowns. By this I mean, we don't know the full extent of his involvement in various operations. For example, as I previously mentioned, Simpson's wife's Facebook post suggests he was responsible for many of the charges in the Steele dossier. He was Steele's boss. Is it possible, then, that some of the sources in the Steele dossier were his sources? It seems likely. By hiring Steele, who had worked with the FBI previously on the FIFA soccer scandal, Simpson now had a second direct conduit to law enforcement—in addition to Ohr at the DOJ.

You can't overestimate the importance of being a known entity to the FBI. The FBI has a process for verifying information from new, unverified sources, but Steele had a documented record with the FBI, which rendered this process largely unnecessary. No hard evidence has surfaced outlining a formal Simpson plan to weaponize Steele's reporting, but that, in effect, is precisely what happened.

Making matters worse was the presence of Rinat Akhmetshin at the Trump Tower meeting. Akhmetshin is a shadowy figure known for lobbying and deep connections to Russian intelligence. But he has admitted to other critical connections, specifically to the Clinton team. How incredibly hypocritical for anti-Trump Clinton acolytes to attack Don Trump Jr. for accepting a meeting with a Russian who proudly professes to be friendly with members of the Clinton staff.

This brings us to the Steele memos themselves.[15] The very first memo is listed as number 080. We know that Steele was hired in June and that first memo was dated June 20. Had Steele written seventy-nine other memos prior to that in the space of a month? Or had the memo-numbering system been initiated by Simpson, who had been working on the Trump collusion and was, per his wife, the driving force behind the dossier? The second memo in the dossier is listed as 086. Again, does this mean there were other memos in between 080 and 086?

These open issues cast further doubt on how Simpson and Steele worked and may suggest that Steele's name and prior reputation with the FBI as an informant served to launder Simpson's handiwork and sourcing. By incorporating intelligence he received from Simpson as his own research—a reality implied by Simpson's wife—Steele may have wittingly or unwittingly served to sanitize and legitimize the fabrications of the "sources" providing the now debunked anti-Trump opposition research.

Adding fuel to the idea that Simpson was behind some of Steele's reporting is the matter of the dossier's sources. The first source to be publicly identified was Sergei Millian, who was outed in a January 24, 2017, *Wall Street Journal* article. Millian was identified as the person referred to at various times as both Source D and Source E, according to a *Journal* informant described as "a person familiar with the matter."[16]

A Belarusian-born resident of Atlanta who speaks six languages and claims to have ties to Trump via lawyer Michael Cohen, Millian seems shadier than a giant oak tree in full summer bloom. George Papadopoulos reports that Millian once offered him $30,000 a month on behalf of an unnamed Russian millionaire—provided the former Trump advisor was part of the administration.[17] In his book, *Deep State Target*, Papadopoulos also says Millian bragged about meeting John McCain during inauguration weekend, and that Millian didn't utter a word of denial when a friend stated, "You know Sergei works for the FBI."[18]

Meanwhile, to really confuse things, Millian was photographed with Oleg Deripaska—the man who lent Manafort $10 million—in the summer of 2016.

So Millian's allegiances are murky, to say the least. And it seems just as likely that the U.S.-based fabricator would have crossed Simpson's orbit—like he would have crossed Steele's. Furthermore, some of the stories about hookers and blackmail while Trump was in Moscow that are attributed to Millian in the dossier seem more likely to have happened—or should I say slightly more plausible?—if they had come from sources with ties to Azerbaijani-Russian billionaire businessman Aras Agalarov—who hosted Trump's 2013 Miss Universe contest—or his son, Emin. But I guess when you are laundering sensationally sleazy fiction, reliable sources are hard to find.

It's entirely possible, given what we know, that Millian was just another plug-and-play piece of Simpson's game, a kind of human quote machine who existed to help Simpson and Steele fabricate sensational fictions—hookers, pee tapes, conspiracies—about Trump, Putin, and Russian intelligence.

While we're on the subject, it's tempting to ask what rules were in place—besides ethics, fair play, and professional decency—to stop Simpson from "piping," as journalists say, his own quotes to Steele and passing them off as sourced.

Simpson has talked about firewalls between his various clients and jobs. But this is a guy who traffics in dirt and damage. He foisted unverified, unproven allegations to the highest reaches of law enforcement. His standards basically amount to, "Trust me."

"I call it journalism for rent," Simpson said while speaking at the 2016 Double Exposure Investigative Film Festival and Symposium, where he described Fusion GPS's work on a panel titled "Investigations with an Agenda."[19]

That's a pretty sleazy description. It almost makes an honorable profession sound like the world's oldest profession. Simpson's motive was Simpson. He was in the business of generating research reports and strategy. For a guy who was critical of Manafort's lobbying and influencing efforts, Simpson wasn't any holy man. His work to undo the Magnitsky Act was in service to the same corrupt and brutal Russian oligarchy that, according to his own DNC research, was a close cousin to the same regime attacking America and supposedly working with the Trump campaign. So it's clear he would work on any issue—even ones that seem to oppose each other. We know he got $1 million from the DNC. We don't know what the Russians paid him for the Magnitsky work. But whatever he got, it looks like dirty money to me.

CHRISTOPHER STEELE

There is no question that the report that bears Christopher Steele's name was central to igniting the Russiagate investigation. Key FBI figures like Andrew McCabe and James Comey have said so, and the dossier dishes heavily on Trump advisor Carter Page, providing the FBI with ammunition to plug into its FISA application on Page and, by extension, the campaign.

What was Steele's motive? The narrative is that he pushed his reporting to agency contacts because he was so alarmed by the material he was gathering. In an interview with the Senate Judicial Committee, Glenn Simpson said Steele was worried that Trump was being blackmailed by Russia and wondered if "this represented a national security threat."

Added Simpson: "He said he thought we were obligated to tell someone in government, in our government, about this information."

Steele has remained largely silent about his work and his methods. Simpson has said another London-based Russia researcher, Edward Baumgartner, worked on the dossier as a subcontractor and reportedly did much of the legwork. But Steele was the front man for the dossier, and he first brought it to the attention of the FBI in July 2016.

Steele is the former head of the MI6 Russia desk, but more than three years after he wrote his initial dossier memos about the hookers, the sleazy video tapes, Michael Cohen's trip to pay off hackers in Prague, and Carter Page and Paul Manafort's working together to ferry secrets to the Trump campaign from Russians, those memos have been entirely debunked. In fact, they seem based on nothing but lies and fantasies.

Steele had been officially out of the spy game for years when he started working on the dossier. Were his contacts stale? Did he have any Russian contacts at all? Or, as he seems to have told Deputy Assistant Secretary of State Kathleen Kavalec in October 2016—ten days before the FBI swore to the first FISA warrant in front of the court—were Steele's sources the Russian intelligence higher-up, Vyacheslav Trubnikov, and

Putin's ideological architect, Vladislav Surkov? Yes, that same Surkov who was once Putin's right-hand man and who publicly proclaimed his penchant for Russian disinformation and interfering in American's brains. What was Steele's budget to pay for information? Were sources telling him what he wanted to hear in return for an easy payday? Were they engaging Steele and Simpson in a sophisticated Russian disinformation campaign designed to sow discord? Who, exactly, were his sources? Who were Baumgartner's?

Whomever the informants were, they were wrong, either intentionally in the case of a disinformation campaign, or unintentionally for various other reasons, including sheer incompetence. And by forwarding their outrageous fictions along, Steele was effectively doing Glenn Simpson's dirty work—laundering bogus reports with his own good-soldier reputation for Trump-hating mainstream consumption. He put his supposedly sterling reputation on the line for $75,000 with shoddy research that detonated the biggest counterintelligence investigation in history. He should have asked Simpson for a raise, given the negative publicity he generated.

Of course, it goes without saying that what he really deserves is to never work again on intelligence matters. He may go to his grave swearing he believes that the garbage he wrote was plausible. But spreading that unverified drivel against Trump and America is potentially criminal and unquestionably unethical and immoral.

ANDREW MCCABE

James Comey named Andrew McCabe deputy director of the FBI in late January 2016. When President Trump fired Comey, asserting his unassailable legal right to appoint the head of the agency, McCabe became the acting director. One of the first things he did was to initiate an investigation into the president on possible charges of obstruction of justice.

He also moved to solidify the Russiagate witch hunt so that it couldn't be closed—despite the shaky evidence behind it. "I wanted to make sure that our case was on solid ground and if somebody came in behind me and closed it and tried to walk away from it, they would not be able to do that without creating a record of why they made that decision," McCabe said.[20]

These moves make perfect sense if you consider that McCabe was loyal to the man who appointed him. But why was McCabe promoted in the first place?

A well-placed FBI source has told me that McCabe was widely known in the agency for his gift of gab, not for his investigative skills in the field as an agent. His reputation wasn't for nabbing bank robbers and hardened criminals. It was for nabbing headlines. He was known as a good "briefer." He was good in front of the camera and for presenting other agents' work to the press and the public.

There's nothing wrong with being a great PR guy—the FBI needs great PR guys now more than ever. (Ironically, hours before McCabe was set to retire, Attorney General Jeff Sessions fired him, claiming McCabe had made an "unauthorized disclosure to the news media and lacked candor." McCabe has denied any wrongdoing and called his termination politically motivated.) But my source cites this as evidence that McCabe is politically savvy. That doesn't mean he wants to get into politics, but he knows how to make things happen—for himself and others. If he only applied the same savvy to actual shoe-leather-type investigative work, then there would be no need to write this book right now.

McCabe's wife, Jill, however, did want to get into politics. In 2015, Jill, a pediatric emergency physician, decided to run for Virginia's state Senate as a Democrat. And she had the blessing of the state's most powerful politician: Terry McAuliffe, who reportedly funneled more than $650,000 to her campaign fund. While that is a tremendous amount of money for a state Senate campaign, the link to McAuliffe is what is essential here.

There are few people in politics with tighter connections to Bill and Hillary Clinton than Terry McAuliffe. He was the Clintons' fundraiser in chief, the man who gathered contributions for the Clintons' campaigns, the William J. Clinton Presidential Library and Museum, and the Clinton's mega-flush foundation. He also reportedly secured the loan for the Clintons' Chappaqua, New York, house—personally!

So let's connect the dots. McCabe's wife, Jill, gets big money from Terry McAuliffe, who is one of Hillary Clinton's best pals, and McCabe formalizes an obstruction-of-justice investigation against the president of the United States, who beat Hillary Clinton.

Anybody see a problem here?

Optics are important, and they cut both ways. The optics, or appearances, surrounding the Trump campaign disturbed many D.C. insiders. Here was a rookie candidate saying some positive things about a new relationship with Russia. He hired a guy with legal issues and questionable ties that nobody flagged—including the same intelligence agencies that had previously identified Manafort's partner during a stint working with the McCain campaign. But how are the optics surrounding McCabe not equally disturbing? Or *more* disturbing?

By running the counterintelligence investigation and investigating Trump for obstruction of justice, McCabe accomplished three things at once:

1. **He repaid a favor to McAuliffe for supporting his wife.**
2. **He helped legitimize the entire Russiagate investigation.**
3. **He kept investigative pressure on Trump—not on the Clintons and their endless stream of scandals.**

JAMES COMEY

Former FBI director James Comey has more motives for spinning Russiagate and keeping the heat on Trump than almost anyone else in the

Collusion Chorus. Let's start with the ancient history: it's easy to forget that one month before the 2016 election, Comey was the most hated man in Washington by Clinton-loving liberals. On October 28, 2016, eleven days before the November 9 national election, Comey quietly informed congressional leaders that he was temporarily reopening the FBI's Hillary Clinton email probe, a decision he made after learning that Clinton consigliere Huma Abedin's convicted pervert husband, Anthony Weiner, had a laptop computer that might have Clinton emails on it. News of the reopened investigation leaked and impacted the election immediately. By resurrecting the mystery of the missing emails, Comey inadvertently put Clinton back in the hot seat and knocked the front-runner off her game.

This botched investigation made Comey public enemy #1 among East Coast power brokers, the media elite and, no doubt, the man who had given him his job: Barack Obama. Democrats were howling for his head! His only path to redemption, then, was Russiagate and undermining Trump. Otherwise, he would be known among the East Coast elite as the clown who handed the election to Trump.

But fortunately for him and unfortunately for the country, Comey's agency underlings allowed a bailout plan to progress. FBI counterintelligence director Peter Strzok opened an investigation into collusion between Trump and the Russians. As we shall see, Strzok, a virulently anti-Trump investigator, did great damage to the probe. And under Comey's watch, Strzok's operation went off the rails, abandoning operational practices and legal requirements in order to push the probe forward.

At a March 20, 2017, hearing, Republican New York congresswoman Elise Stefanik nailed Comey for ignoring established protocol. After getting Comey to admit that the FBI typically informs congressional leaders about high-profile investigations every quarter, she asked why the agency waited more than six months to provide a briefing on the Russia–Trump investigation.

"It was a matter of such sensitivity that we wouldn't include it in the quarterly briefings," Comey said during the hearing.[21]

Remember, when Comey went and briefed the president-elect in Trump Tower, he called the charges "salacious and unverified"—words that suggest he doubted the veracity of the allegations.

For the FBI to proceed with a FISA warrant request to spy on American citizens, they must follow the Woods Procedures. These are FISA verification rules named after Michael Woods, a former member of the FBI's general counsel.

In 2003, then FBI director Robert Mueller described the Woods Procedures in a letter to Senator Patrick Leahy. Among the many notable things Mueller revealed—including how previous FISA applications contained inaccuracies and failed to note relevant details, such as one FISA target's being a former informant—is: "The Woods procedures are used to ensure the accuracy of the information contained in the declaration."[22]

Mueller went on: "By signing and swearing to the declaration, the headquarters agent is attesting to the knowledge of what is contained in the declaration."

The agent's name is redacted in the FISA request to spy on Carter Page that was granted on October 21, 2016. But the heavily redacted FISA application clearly has James Comey's signature on page sixty-eight, certifying that the execution of the document was "in accordance with the requirements of the Foreign Intelligence Surveillance Act of 1978, as amended." By signing, Comey was stating that the application complied with the Woods Procedures. But it didn't.

There are strong indications that not everything was on the up-and-up. We now know that convicted Russian spies had concluded that Page wasn't spy material—they even called Page an "idiot." And we know that Carter Page had assisted our intelligence community in the apprehension of Russian spies in the past.[23] We know that Christopher Steele, the allegedly "reliable source" of the "verified" FISA information, couldn't keep his own story straight when he told Kathleen Kavalec of the State Department that Michael Cohen had traveled to Prague to coordinate the collusion scheme—yet just eight days later, Steele wrote a dossier memo to the FBI saying that his sources were "unsure" of the location of the Cohen meeting. Kind of a big detail to "forget," no? We know that Steele told Kavalec that he wanted his information out before Election Day, obviously indicating that his motives were political, not related to security. We also know, thanks to Kavalec's notes, that Steele mentioned Trubnikov and Surkov, two Putin allies with expertise in Russian disinformation, while discussing sources.

This evidence would have completely undercut the request in front of the FISA court, but no one at the court was ever notified about it. It was likely never included in the original FISA or the three FISA warrant renewals, although some of the warrant[24] remains redacted. At least one published report, however, says that this is exactly what happened. Citing "congressional sources who have seen the unredacted document," *Real Clear Investigations* reports that "the FBI omitted from its application to spy on Carter Page the fact that Russian spies had dismissed the former Trump campaign adviser as unreliable."[25]

One more *huge* point was apparently excluded from the FISA warrant: that Steele was being paid by the Hillary Clinton team and the DNC. Glenn Simpson's bill may have been paid by Perkins Coie lawyers, but the Clinton campaign and the DNC were paying the law firm. The original FISA warrant fails to reveal that specific connection, and simply states, "Source #1 [Steele]…was approached by an identified U.S. person [Simpson], who indicated to Source #1 that a U.S. law firm had hired the identified U.S. person to conduct research regarding Candidate #1's [Trump's] ties to Russia."[26]

Everybody got that? Steele was approached by Simpson, who told him a law firm wanted Trump-Russia dirt. Simple, right?

But the deeper reality has been ignored. Here's the rest of the FBI's not-so-full disclosure:

(The identified U.S. Person and Source #1 have a longstanding business relationship.) The identified U.S. person hired Source #1 to conduct this research. The identified U.S. Person never advised Source #1 as to the motivation behind the research into Candidate #1's ties to Russia. The FBI speculates that the identified U.S. Person was likely looking for information that could be used to discredit Candidate #1's campaign.[27]

Shouldn't a judge have been presented with the fact that the source had been indirectly paid by Hillary Clinton, the opponent of the man for whom FISA target Carter Page worked?

Additionally, I have one more reason to believe that Comey signed at least one FISA warrant in bad faith. A well-placed insider on Capitol Hill has assured me that an FBI agent interviewed one of Christopher Steele's Russian subsources and wrote up a 302—the FBI designation for an interview summary—that indicated the informant was untrustworthy and not telling the truth. According to my insider, Comey had seen the 302 or been told about it by January 2017 at the latest.

If this is true—and I believe it is—then Comey would seem to have violated the strict Woods Procedures. These FISA protocols require the inclusion of any information that might change the court's view of a warrant. Because it was not mentioned that an FBI agent had discovered that one of Steele's subsources was lying, these procedures were clearly violated.

The first FISA renewal occurred in January 2017, so we don't know if Comey had heard this damning evaluation before signing off on that document. But he did sign off on April's FISA with nary a mention of this. Why would he do that? He needed to keep the warrant open to investigate and impinge on the Trump presidency, *not* to investigate "collusion," which he assuredly knew at this point was a hoax.

To be clear, Comey and his team needed the FISA warrant because it allowed the agency to spy not only on Page, but on anyone Page was in contact with—like those working on the Trump campaign—through the "two-hop rule," a constitutional abnormality that allows the recipients of a FISA warrant to encircle almost anyone in a target's entire network. In this case, that meant nearly everyone in the Trump campaign.

So the FISA declarations were fundamentally flawed, inaccurate, and in some cases easily debunked (such as the allegation that Michael Cohen went to Prague, and the failure to connect Simpson and Steele's tainted research to the DNC and the Clinton campaign). Yet Comey's team continued skirting FBI norms and procedures and playing fast and loose, failing to identify the connection between Simpson and Candidate #1's (Trump's) rival—Hillary Clinton's campaign and the DNC!

Speaking of playing fast and loose and abusing power, on December 13, 2018, Comey appeared on MSNBC and fragged himself by dropping the bombshell that he had sent FBI agents to the White House to interview National Security Advisor Michael Flynn.

Sleazy Comey admitted that the interview had been arranged directly with Flynn and not through the White House counsel's office. The hardball move—a kind of investigative drive-by—was, according to Comey, "something I probably wouldn't have done or maybe gotten away with in a more…organized administration."[28]

"Gotten away with?"

The director of the FBI, with the power to ruin someone's life and reputation, admits he pulled a fast one on the Trump administration. By getting Flynn to agree to an interview without his lawyers, the national security advisor walked right into Legal Jeopardy 101. And who masterminded that? James "Gotcha" Comey.

With all this malfeasance and all these anti-Trump maneuvers emanating from his office, Comey needed to keep the pressure on the president and off of himself. This is a guiding principle of many of the conflicted members of the Collusion Chorus. Their own records are so slimy and tainted that they resort to the oldest warfare strategy known to man: the best defense is a good offense.

ROD ROSENSTEIN

From almost the moment the Senate confirmed him as the deputy attorney general of the DOJ on April 25, 2017, Rod Rosenstein has been a flashpoint in Russiagate, the unlikely pivot man around which the plans to take down the president have kept swirling.

Rosenstein wrote the memo that the White House used to justify the May 9, 2017, firing of James Comey. "I wrote it. I believe it. I stand by it," he later told Congress.[29] But he wasn't happy about it, according to Andrew McCabe, who described Rosenstein as "glassy-eyed."

"He said it wasn't his idea. The president had ordered him to write the memo justifying the firing," McCabe writes in his book, *The Threat.* He also says Rosenstein feared he was being used by the Trump administration as a scapegoat for Comey's firing.[30]

As if that weren't enough excitement for his first weeks on the job, Rosenstein was also courting Robert Mueller to be Russiagate's special counsel. At around the same time, Mueller's name had reportedly landed on a list of possible candidates to replace Comey as FBI director, and the former G-man was called into the Oval Office to meet the president and Jeff Sessions.

The official story is that this was a job interview. But I smell a rat. I believe it was a job interview for the gig Rosenstein was offering.

Think about it: Mueller was Rosenstein's old boss. They worked together when Rosenstein was an intern in the U.S. Attorney's Office in Boston where Mueller was the interim U.S. attorney. Then they worked together when Mueller headed the criminal division of the DOJ. They are associates. And being dragged into the "fire Comey" memo, Rosenstein was likely horrified by the outsider in the White House. Can't you see it? He wanted his classic Washington, allegedly straight-arrow FBI buddy—Mueller—to witness the upheaval himself. Trump is all passion and gut instincts. Mueller is a cold, calculating, conservative Washington insider. Rosenstein knew that Mueller would think Trump was trouble for their cabal. He knew Mueller would view the job as saving America and sign on.

And that is exactly what happened.

Mueller never told the president or Jeff Sessions, who was also on hand, that he was considering another gig. The very next day, conveniently, Rosenstein announced that Mueller was the new special counsel.

This was a slap in the president's face. Rosenstein didn't just suddenly wake up that morning and say, "Hey, Bob, I just decided to make you the special investigator!" They had to have been planning it for a while.

It's likely that Mueller wanted to meet the president. Otherwise, the professional thing to do would have been to delay that Oval Office meeting. But talking to Trump was probably a deal-clincher. After viewing his polar opposite inhabiting the White House, Mueller probably said, "Sign me up!"

But the real controversy for Rosenstein is that he signed off on the last renewal of the original Russiagate FISA warrant. (FISA warrants expire after ninety days. If you want an extension to spy on suspected foreign agents, a new application must be submitted for each renewal.)

Here's the catch: when the FISA warrant was first renewed and signed by Comey in January 2017, it must have been pretty clear that those juicy details provided by the merchants of dishonesty, Simpson and Steele, were actually garbage. The FBI interviewed one of Steele's "sources" and determined that the source was illegitimate. Steele seems to have admitted to Kavalec that he used Russian disinformation specialists as sources, and Steele couldn't remember his own story with regard to Cohen's infamous Prague trip. Sergei Millian had been exposed as a charlatan who promoted his nonexistent ties to Trump. Michael Cohen denied he had ever been to Prague and offered his passport as evidence. (Note: News source McClatchy reported on December 27, 2018, that evidence had been shared with Mueller indicating that Cohen's cell phone was detected in Prague. This has not been reported anywhere else. It sure would be nice if Simpson and Steele revealed their "sources" who fed them bad information.) The supposed *kompromat* (compromising information) never materialized. And Simpson and Steele's connections to the DNC and Clinton were uncovered.

Rule thirteen of FISA regulations states: "If the government discovers that a submission to the Court contained a misstatement or omission of material fact, the government, in writing, must immediately inform the Judge to whom the submission was made."[31]

Because of the redactions in the three FISA renewals, we don't know all of the adjustments that were made. But if, in late spring 2017, Rosenstein and his crew failed to update the document with exculpatory evidence, then they violated the Woods Procedures, which are integrated into the FISA application requirement.

There were any number of reasons the DOJ and the FBI would want to continue playing fast and loose with the FISA applications. Chief among them is the idea that this was a gamble—that the investigation would be able to produce proof of collusion by pressuring suspects like Papadopoulos, Flynn, Manafort, and longtime Trump advisor Roger Stone to turn over evidence to the witch hunters. Second, Rosenstein (and Comey and Mueller) needed to double down on the previous filing to avoid getting caught in violating the Woods Procedures. Third, as loyal members of the entrenched establishment class, they wanted to destabilize the Trump administration and keep it on the defensive. And fourth, they needed to hide the parallel construction scheme they were conducting. It's now clear that CIA director John Brennan was abusing his intelligence powers in order to spy on the Trump team, and he pushed for the FBI to open a formal probe into the Trump team because he had no power to do so himself. The CIA largely stays away from domestic spying except under exceptional circumstances. But the FBI has no such restrictions. By hiding the likely origins of his information on Trump (some of which was clearly Steele's), Brennan led lawmakers and the FBI to believe that the Steele and Simpson information was being corroborated when, in fact, it was simply being repeated.

Keeping the damning Russiagate shadow in place tainted Trump's election victory and took a toll on his political capital. Russiagate and all the investigation leaks also provided great talking points for damaging Republicans in a critical midterm election—in which electing enough representatives and Senators to impeach the president and remove him from office on the false collusion charges—would be key. And so Rosenstein appointed Robert Mueller, his hero and brother in arms, special counsel so he could continue inflicting damage. As I explain later, Rosenstein even expanded the scope of the investigation to let Mueller run wild.

When Rosenstein appointed Mueller as special counsel, he issued a May 17, 2017, "Appointment of Special Counsel" scope memo authorizing the new hire to investigate "any links or coordination between the Russian government and individuals associated with the campaign of Donald Trump and (2) any matters that arose or may arise directly from that investigation." Three months later, on August 2, he issued a second scope memo, which provided "a more specific description" of the special counsel's authority and revealed detailed allegations against... well, that's the problem. More than half the memo has been redacted, but we now know, due to the release of the Mueller report, that Rosenstein expanded Mueller's investigation to include "allegations that three Trump campaign officials—Carter Page, Paul Manafort, and George Papadopoulos 'committed a crime or crimes by colluding with Russian government officials with respect to the Russian government's efforts to interfere with the 2016 presidential election.'"[32] These claims are made only in Simpson and Steele's dossier information. What the heck was Mueller doing investigating an information stream from discredited sources whom, no later than January 2017, the FBI knew to be illegitimate? He was covering Rosenstein's behind because Rosenstein had signed one of the FISA warrant renewals based on the dirty information, and there was still hope they could salvage the garbage allegations from garbage sources.

Rosenstein has other skeletons in his closet, too. He was the pros-
ecuting United States attorney in the 2015 case involving TENEX, a
company involved in the sale of uranium to Russia. And sources have
told me he was less than aggressive in looking for links between APCO
Worldwide, a lobbyist firm that worked for both TENEX and the Clinton
Foundation. APCO denies that those accounts intersected. But it's
curious that examining spurious Trump-Russia intersections merits a
multimillion-dollar, 600-plus-day investigation, while Clinton involvement in uranium sales to a noted geopolitical foe merits nothing more
than dismissive whispers of "conspiracy theory" by the liberal media.

ROBERT MUELLER

As I mentioned earlier, so much of what spurred Russiagate was the
weaponization of our intelligence and law enforcement community to
investigate poor judgment or bad optics—basically the appearance of
connections that might look suspicious on the outside but evaporate on
closer inspection. Yet nobody seems to have given a damn about optics
when it came to the team of investigators that Special Counsel Robert
Mueller called in to get the goods on Trump.

I believe part of that has to do with Mueller's aura. As the former
FBI director, he has the impressive, no-nonsense image of the ultimate
G-man. He's the second-longest-serving director (2001 to 2013) in FBI
history, after J. Edgar Hoover, and has a reputation as a straight shooter,
a law-and-order guy who worked for George W. Bush and Obama. So it
sure seemed that Rosenstein had brought in the ultimate company man
to give the appearance that the FBI and the DOJ were beyond reproach.

But his hires all came with tremendous baggage that anyone with an
internet connection could've uncovered. While the mainstream media
hailed some of the special counsel's hires as members of a prosecutorial
dream team, they conveniently overlooked—or even gushed about—
dubious connections.

Jeannie Rhee worked at Mueller's previous law firm, WilmerHale. Her previous clients not only included the Clinton Foundation, but she also represented former secretary of state Hillary Clinton in a lawsuit seeking access to her private emails. It's no wonder she donated $5,400 to Clinton in 2015 and 2016.

Andrew Weissmann was Mueller's mad-dog lieutenant, notorious for his ethical lapses, poor attitude, and take-no-prisoners prosecutions—like with the team that investigated the Enron Corporation collapse and earned over thirty convictions. But these cases were often brutal affairs, and even when Weissmann won—getting a conviction for Enron auditor Arthur Andersen—he often lost, like when the Supreme Court overturned that high-profile verdict.

Weissmann has also drawn heat for a fan letter he wrote to acting Attorney General Sally Yates after she instructed the Justice Department not to defend President Donald Trump's ban on travelers from several nations with pronounced terrorism problems. Trump fired her, but Weissmann sent Yates a sycophantic note for defying the president: "I am so proud and in awe. Thank you so much. All my deepest respect."[33] Making matters worse, Mueller left Weissmann in charge of hiring the members of the special counsel team, virtually ensuring a brigade of anti-Trump hostiles.

With clear-cut Obama and Clinton loyalists on the team, the optics should have been a concern. As it turns out, they were more a dream team for chaos than law and order. The case against Roger Stone remains untried. But so far, except for Manafort, the legal wins these top prosecutors have obtained amount to one big yawn. And those wins certainly have *nothing* to do with colluding with Russians.

Mueller, alleged law-and-order icon that he is, appears to have been in lockstep with Rosenstein. As such, he was the key man in carrying out the investigation's objectives and fulfilling the mission detailed in the scope memo and the cryptic addition to the scope memo. So even though he has been a silent character, the tightest-lipped poker player at the table, we'll be focusing on Mueller a lot. His motives began with the impression that he was going to save the country. But that evidently changed when he realized he had become the FBI's partner in slime. He had to save both the FBI's reputation and his own—not to mention Rosenstein's and everyone else's who had gotten suckered into a federally funded witch hunt.

CHAPTER 3

Plan A: Ad-Libbing Adversaries

The war to take down Trump before and after the election wasn't a conspiracy with a single puppet master pulling all of the strings. It evolved out of a confluence of events: a cabal of power-crazed Democrats; foreign intelligence operations; efforts by the Russians to sow disinformation; and, most critically, a dangerous kind of Washington-based groupthink that infected the mainstream media with heavily politicized misinformation. Eventually, these elements solidified into a dirty game of information laundering and a plot to fabricate the appearance of Russian collusion—a conspiracy to fake a conspiracy, really. But there was never a single wizard of Washington, a sinister Mr. Big, calling all the shots.

So forget it; this was not a Hollywood movie plot with a cigar-smoking shadowy figure orchestrating every nuanced media hit, every FBI leak, every indictment. That's the same kind of thinking that created the unfounded paranoia about Trump. As the results of the special counsel's absurd $35 million investigation prove, Trump isn't in Putin's pocket. He wasn't plotting with Russians to steal an election. He didn't try to put together a network of bad actors to commit what would have amounted to treason. No, it's the Obama administration that had access to that kind of stuff—seventeen intelligence agencies, in fact, all capable of running various special ops. Obama headed a government with literally thousands of intelligence and law enforcement experts trained in surveillance, data collection, and counterintelligence. Trump? He had a small private security team and a now-disgraced lawyer named Michael Cohen, a guy who Trump and the rest of the world now know had delusions of grandeur and big legal problems. Those were Trump's guys when it came to navigating any nefarious activity. End of story. Trump was too damn busy running a presidential campaign as a rookie candidate to carry out some elaborate pie-in-the-sky Russian collusion plot. And judging by his crowds and poll numbers, he didn't need to. (It is not widely known, but Patrick Caddell, the late pollster who masterminded Jimmy Carter's and Ross Perot's campaigns, predicted Trump would win based on a series of polls he had conducted in 2016. As America headed to the polls, Caddell ran into media mogul Rupert Murdoch at Fox News and told him that Trump would win, thanks to an electorate utterly disgusted with the privileged ruling elite.)

And while Glenn Simpson concocted the plug-and-play strategy to weaponize "information" and feed it to the FBI, he did not single-handedly move all the central players of Russiagate into position like some evil-genius chess master. Believe me, I would love to say that's the case—because what a story that would be. But easy explanations are typically the hallmarks of ridiculous conspiracy theories, and what actually happened is complicated but understandable.

So what I call Plan A wasn't really a plan at first. It took time to gestate. The real conspiracy—the plot to tar Trump—emerged out of chaos: out of the muck from the swamp that Washington had become; out of an Obama administration accustomed to weaponizing its substantial intelligence powers to target its political opponents; out of a media atmosphere entirely incapable of honestly reporting on the Obama administration; and, finally, out of a city divided by partisan politics, by the endless quest for power and influence, and by a stunning lack of accountability when it comes to the abuse of power. The end of the Obama administration was an ugly time in America. The Republican-controlled Senate had essentially stripped the president of his power, acting to check his liberal agenda. The country was at a political impasse.

Meanwhile, investigations into scandals surrounding his administration were stagnant, stalled, or swept under the rug. And the central figure in a boatload of those scandals, Hillary Clinton, appeared to be Teflon-coated. Not only did she avoid any penalties for her mishandling of the Benghazi terror attacks, for abusing national security laws regarding the use of a private email server, and for trading political access and favors for money for herself and the Clinton Foundation, but she seemed to think she would waltz into the White House.

The idea that Clinton might lose, that the prevailing power structure that had been in place for eight years might shift, that those in leadership positions might be called into account, and that the lords of the swamp might be evicted was a frightening one. New administrations have the right to clean house. But a Trump win wouldn't just threaten job security for a couple of generational insiders and their next of kin; it would upend the entire broken system. As we've seen, some Republicans were calling for Obama's intelligence guru James Clapper to face charges for lying to Congress. For Comey, who had botched the Clinton investigation, his career and reputation were at stake—some critics wanted his head for giving Clinton's email abuses a pass, while Democrats wanted him tarred and feathered for reopening the email investigation eleven days before the presidential election. And plenty of other appointees, we now know, could have been called onto the carpet for violating privacy norms and for out-and-out lying to the American people.

At some point, Obama administration officials got very nervous and began ramping up the pressure on the Trump campaign team. "I have seen intelligence reports that clearly show that the president-elect and his team were, I guess, at least monitored," House intelligence chairman Devin Nunes revealed.[1]

And who was doing the monitoring and spilling the beans about it? Just before Trump took over the White House, the offices of both National Security Advisor Susan Rice and United Nations ambassador Samantha Power made requests to unmask (that is, to reveal) the identities of Trump team members—American citizens—who were under surveillance, according to numerous reports. "Power was believed to have made 'hundreds' of unmasking requests to identify individuals named in classified intelligence community reports related to Trump and his presidential transition team," reports the *Free Beacon*.[2]

As for Rice, she is rumored to have provided media with allegations regarding Michael Flynn, her replacement to head the National Security Council (NSC). Of course, when PBS anchor Judy Woodruff asked Rice if she knew anything about individuals on the Trump team's having their identities disclosed, Obama's right-hand woman on national security said, "I know nothing about this. I was surprised to see reports from Chairman Nunes on that count today."

If you buy that story, I've got a bridge in Brooklyn I'd like to sell you at a discount.

According to CNN, multiple sources relayed that Rice "privately told House investigators that she unmasked the identities of senior Trump officials to understand why the crown prince of the United Arab Emirates was in New York late last year."[3]

As both James Comey and former NSA head Mike Rogers testified before the House Intelligence Committee on March 20, 2017, there are only twenty people in the federal government with the authority to approve unmasking requests regarding names that surface in NSA data collection—and all those requests at the time would have been vetted by Rogers, a longtime cyberwar expert appointed to his position by President Obama in 2014.

So the politicization and vilification of the Trump team were in full effect during the transition. But those things had been going on for a full year in subtler, more secretive forms. James Clapper and John Brennan had been stirring the pot, too. But what stoked them into action? New evidence has now surfaced establishing other events that made conditions ripe to launch the plan to take down Donald Trump.

So let's go back in time, back to before Mueller became special counsel, before anyone had heard the names George Papadopoulos, Christopher Steele, and Glenn Simpson.

THE SPIES THAT BLIND

On April 23, 2012, Eric Holder, the U.S. attorney general of the United States, submitted a motion to the Foreign Intelligence Surveillance Court. The seventy-page request sought to expand the FBI's ability to receive information from foreign intelligence services about U.S. citizens who were subject to FISA warrants, or whose names had surfaced during the course of a FISA warrant investigation.[4]

By definition, the motion also sought to allow the FBI to share information about U.S. citizens with foreign partners. Without sharing some identifying information—a name, a profession, a photo—the FBI had no way to obtain information about specific subjects from the foreign governments whose help they were seeking.

So the Obama administration didn't mince words. The motion proposed that "the following underlined text will be inserted into the first sentence: 'The FBI may disseminate FISA-acquired information concerning United States persons, which reasonably appears to be foreign intelligence information, is necessary to understand foreign intelligence information or assess its importance, or is evidence of a crime being disseminated for a law enforcement purpose, to foreign governments as follows...'"[5]

The wording was broad and fuzzy.

"'Reasonably necessary to understand foreign intelligence or assess its importance?' That's pretty vague," Republican Texas congressman Louie Gohmert told the *Daily Caller* in April 2019. "There's nothing they could obtain on American citizens that John Brennan or James Clapper couldn't say 'it helped me understand other intelligence.'"[6]

The motion passed. It became part of FISA law.

Back in 2012, Obama's legal eagles obviously weren't planning to spy specifically on Donald Trump or anyone in his presidential campaign—he hadn't even declared his candidacy. But the move, couched in language about combating international and domestic terrorism threats, established a precedent for spies to exchange information. It greased the wheels for the hostile operation that would unfold as Trump's rise to power became more of a threat.

The motion also established that the FBI's tentacles extend beyond American borders. The bureau works with foreign intelligence organizations as a matter of course. And this new language would prove vital to manufacturing Russiagate.

POISONED SOURCES

The 2012 FISA rules update also suggests the extent to which intelligence collection had become one big game of unvetted show and tell. Obviously, in the age of Islamic terrorism and murderous organizations like ISIS and Al Qaeda urging rogue attacks on the West, we want intelligence agencies to share information about bad actors. But who, exactly, is identifying bad actors and who, exactly, is verifying the information about "persons of interest"? It can be a slippery slope.

In terms of the Trump campaign, the slope was about as slippery as a sheet of ice greased with melted butter. How allegations surfaced against the Trump campaign is still mystifying, but the story has all the markings of a thirsty Obama administration and an all-too-eager-to-comply Russian disinformation bartender.

We know a good deal about Glenn Simpson and his plug-and-play template.

We know that George Papadopoulos was approached by Maltese professor Joseph Mifsud in Italy back on March 12, 2016. About six weeks later, on April 26, Mifsud allegedly told Papadopoulos about "thousands of emails" that the Russian had.[7]

We know that Australian high commissioner Alexander Downer, a proud pal of Bill Clinton's, claims that Papadopoulos told him the Russians had dirt on Hillary Clinton—something Papadopoulos denies ever doing.[8]

And we know that Downer's recounting of that alleged incident is what the FBI *claims* ignited the Crossfire Hurricane counterintelligence operation, which launched on July 31, 2016.

A number of questions, however, have developed over this last point. Downer has been clear that Papadopoulos never mentioned emails during their conversation—and yet, somehow, according to the *New York Times*' initial report, the FBI learned that Mifsud had mentioned emails to Papadopoulos. So if FBI agents knew this as noted in their FISA warrant, who told them?

There are several possibilities. In Papadopoulos's book, he admits to telling Greek foreign minister Nikolaos Kotzias about the emails.[9] Was that meeting under surveillance? Or did Kotzias, who has close ties to Moscow, share the info with the U.S.? Another possible source of the email story, of course, is Mifsud himself and his handlers.

But we still don't know conclusively whom Mifsud was working for (although all signs point strongly to Mifsud's being a Western intelligence asset), who fed him the hacking information, or if that tale was just another of the many fabrications he spun for Papadopoulos. It seems unlikely that Mifsud was a Russian asset, given that Papadopoulos has repeatedly said Mifsud succeeded in introducing him only to two alleged Russians of little consequence, and that one of them was a young woman whom Mifsud introduced as Putin's niece—even though Putin doesn't have a niece. So whom was the mysterious Mifsud working for, and what was his end game? Because if Mifsud was not a Russian intelligence asset, as the Russian collusion hoaxsters insist, then we are likely looking at an entrapment scheme marshaled by intelligence agencies supposedly friendly to U.S. interests. That's right: a setup.

The FBI actually asked Papadopoulos for Mifsud's contact information during an interview. The agency also reportedly interviewed Mifsud when he came to a State Department-sponsored conference.[10] Suspiciously, FISA warrant applications made after the FBI's February 2017 interview with Mifsud do not seem to have been updated with what, if anything, that interview revealed. This is strange considering that Mifsud's alleged proclamations to Papadopoulos about the Russians' having information about emails are what, according to the shady FBI explanation, kick-started the FBI's investigation into the Trump team.

It is hard not to look at all this circumstantial evidence and wonder if our British pals were either duped or actively trying to fool U.S. intelligence. The very first whispers of Trump's being entwined with Russia, not coincidentally, emanated from London. The *Guardian* reports that in late 2015, Britain's Government Communications Headquarters (GCHQ), the nation's eavesdropping agency, was listening in on Moscow targets when these "known Kremlin operatives" were picked up talking to people associated with Trump. The precise details revealed during these alleged recorded exchanges have not been made public. But the intelligence was sent to U.S. agencies.[11]

As for more curious British connections, Downer, one of the most senior foreign diplomats in London, and ex-MI6 director Richard Dearlove (who, ironically, vouched for Steele's Russian-intelligence-gathering abilities to the media) both sat on the board of directors of Hakluyt & Co., one of the world's leading private intelligence groups, based in the U.K. George Papadopoulos had been working in England at the London Centre of International Law Practice when he was steered to meet Mifsud in Rome by, according to Papadopoulos, Arvinder Sambei, whom he refers to as "the legal counsel for the FBI in the U.K. who just happens to be a director at this organization."[12] It should be noted that Sambei challenged this description of events in an interview with T. A. Frank in the *Washington Post*, in which she said she was "completely taken aback" because she claims she met Papadopoulos only once.[13] In addition, she is a former senior prosecutor at the Crown Prosecution Service, where, she claims, she worked with the FBI but was never employed as counsel. Mifsud had worked in London previously and eventually joined the same firm, the London Centre of International Law Practice, where Papadopoulos worked. That Papadopoulos and Mifsud, two incidental characters almost entirely off the radar in terms of notoriety, became the crux of the biggest political espionage scandal in modern history would be inconceivable except for two things.

First, Papadopoulos was the ideal target, according to anyone familiar with Black Ops 101. He was young, ambitious, and inexperienced—a vulnerable combination to exploit for masters of spycraft—and he had access to the Trump campaign.

Second, Mifsud had a dirty past, reportedly spiked with at least two money scandals and one now-defunct school, the London Academy of Diplomacy.[14] So he might easily be enticed to spin the young American target.

It seems beyond obvious that somebody with a grudge against the Trump team decided to use these two guys to effectively plant a virus inside the Trump campaign that could grow into Russian collusion charges.

Fortunately for Papadopoulos, he didn't bite.

Unfortunately for Papadopoulos, the FBI did.

Meanwhile, on December 28, 2015, Peter Strzok, chief of the FBI's counterespionage section, sent a text to his FBI coworker and girlfriend, Lisa Page, a member of the FBI's general counsel office. Strzok asked if she had "all our oconus lures approved?"[15] OCONUS is an acronym most frequently used by the military to mean "outside the continental

United States." In other words, Strzok was asking about foreign spies or overseas informants. No smoking-gun texts have surfaced that reveal which agents Strzok was referring to or what their missions were. But the exchange by two senior FBI employees who were later found to harbor disturbing anti-Trump biases that got them bounced off the Mueller investigative team and its timing—just after the GCHQ informed the U.S. of noise about Trump and Russia—remain incredibly suspicious.

According to the unofficial narrative of mainstream media, the GCHQ reports didn't send off immediate shock waves. U.S. intelligence agencies regarded the communiqués with caution, apparently, because they can't—legally, anyway—examine private communications of U.S. citizens without a warrant. But there are ways around this. They are called intelligence summaries. The foreign intelligence agents simply outline the content of their intercepts. Were Strzok's lures related to that GCHQ report? File that with the known unknowns. But about six months later, the GCHQ was so worried about perceived inaction by U.S. intelligence that the British agency's then-head, Robert Hannigan, flew to the U.S. to meet John Brennan and deliver his ominous Trump-related news personally.[16]

Add Christopher Steele's approaching an FBI agent in Rome, also during the summer of 2016, and the international intelligence agency chatter—German, French, and Dutch spies also reportedly chimed in—was coming from all directions. All of it cast a mountain of aspersions on Trump and the campaign.

Was any of it verified?

Not a single word.

Why let facts get in the way of an investigation into the one man who could burn the wretched swamp to the ground?

By late summer of 2016, as Trump and Hillary Clinton were going into the homestretch as their respective party nominees, that chatter—about Russian meddling, about Russian *kompromat*, and about Trump associates in contact with Kremlin operatives—had landed in the ears of Brennan, Clapper, and Comey. Three of America's top intelligence figures, all Obama loyalists, had been saturated with unconfirmed reports of alleged misdeeds by Trump team members. While we know that Glenn Simpson and Christopher Steele had targeted the FBI and Comey, the facts around the foreign-fed "intelligence" given to Brennan and then presumably shared with Clapper remain murky. We don't know what the CIA director was told. But the explosive notes of the October 11, 2016, meeting between the U.S. State Department's Kathleen Kavalec and Steele, which surfaced in May 2019, provide some clues. Steele met with Kavalec *before* the FBI swore to the information in the FISA warrant application just a few weeks later—and, during a discussion of his "sources," dropped the names of Russian disinformation specialists Trubnikov and Surkov. Since Steele was trying to convince Kavalec that his reports were legitimate, it seems highly likely that these were his sources.

Interestingly, Trubnikov was an associate of Stefan Halper, the U.S. spy who probed the Trump team through his contacts with Papadopoulos and Carter Page, at the Cambridge Intelligence Seminar. Halper actually taught classes with Trubnikov at the University of Cambridge in the U.K. Halper was also close with Richard Dearlove, the former U.K. spy chief. Both Dearlove and Halper suspiciously resigned from the Cambridge Intelligence Seminar shortly after the upset 2016 election victory of Donald Trump, stating, unbelievably, that the victory was due to "unacceptable Russian influence." Whose influence? Trubnikov's?

Dearlove and Halper were also at the July 2016 event at—guess where?—Cambridge, to which Halper had invited the target of the October 2016 FISA warrant, Trump team member Carter Page.

The CIA, headed by political opportunist John Brennan, would assuredly have been aware of contacts between a well-known U.S. human intelligence asset such as Halper, on foreign soil and in a foreign country, and associates of the Republican nominee for the U.S. presidency. It appears likely that Brennan was running a rogue intelligence-gathering

operation, which would explain GOP congressman Devin Nunes's assertion that no "official" intelligence was used to open the investigation into
Trump. A good source of "unofficial" intelligence would've been Trubnikov, Halper, and Dearlove's troika, which used conduit Christopher
Steele to circumvent traditional intelligence channels and to pipeline the
unverified, salacious allegations directly to John Brennan. The CIA chief
could then pass them off to ethically compromised politicians, such as
Harry Reid, who would then push them to the FBI. Voilà! Then the FBI
could say that the information they, along with the DNC and Hillary
Clinton, were paying for from Steele was verified! Although, again, it
was just being repeated, *not* verified.

Brennan has some explaining to do and he knows it. The self-ap-
pointed anti-Trump cheerleader ever so slightly toned down his act in
the wake of the Mueller report. The lack of criminal charges from the
special counsel evidently caused a brief moment of reflection about his
idiotic tweets. Unfortunately, he didn't get very far with his introspection.

"I don't know if I received bad information, but I think I suspected
there was more than there actually was," Brennan told MSNBC host
Joe Scarborough on March 25, 2019, one day after Attorney General
William Barr announced that Mueller had found no evidence of the
Trump campaign's colluding with Russia.[17]

What does Brennan's mystifying, nonapology mean? Let me try to
translate: Brennan was unsure about the factual accuracy of the information he received as head of the CIA regarding Russiagate—even
though he used that information to support a crippling investigation
against Donald Trump and his team. And the reason he didn't have any
problem cheerleading and slinging mud against Trump on behalf of the
election's sore losers is that he had a hunch that more information would
be uncovered that would condemn Trump. Unfortunately for Brennan,
his hunch—something commonly known as wishful thinking—was a
total bust. So his statement conveyed this without actually admitting he
was wrong.

It is stunning that America's spy chief had this hunch based on his rogue intelligence operation while others investigating the matter had grave doubts. Even Peter Strzok, the now disgraced FBI counterintelligence guru and self-proclaimed Trump hater, shared his private misgivings about proving allegations of collusion, texting his lover Lisa Page that "my gut sense and concern is there's no big there there." Strzok wrote that message on May 18, 2017, as he moved to join the special counsel's team. As Page later explained at a congressional hearing, Strzok was voicing doubt about what the investigation would uncover. "It still existed in the scope of possibility that there would be literally nothing" to connect Trump and Russia, no matter what Mueller or the FBI did.[18]

In other words, two of the members of Mueller's original investigative team, both of whom were familiar with the FBI investigation on a granular level—an investigation that had been ongoing for nine months—were discussing the fact that no misdeeds had been uncovered. These texts essentially exonerated Trump before the Mueller probe was officially set in motion. And yet that investigation went full steam ahead.

The whole thing is more remarkable when you consider that Strzok despised Trump. Texts he sent Page reveal that he called the future president an "idiot," an "enormous douche" and "a f***ing idiot."[19] If he had found an iota of evidence that implicated Trump or Trump campaign members, he would have been all over it. Yet, despite his sneering contempt, we know that after leading the FBI investigation for months, he admitted in private that the bureau had turned up nothing tying Trump or his campaign to Russia.

And that leads us back to Brennan. What could he have possibly learned that Strzok hadn't? Until the CIA honcho shares those allegations and the sources, we won't be able to close the case. But given the substantial amount we do know, it seems clear that either he got spun like a top by a Russian disinformation campaign and was led to smear and destabilize the Trump presidency because of it, or he just had it out for the president of the United States and was too emotionally unstable to control his tyrannical impulses.

FORESHADOWING FLYNN

Before we wrap up the inventory of this bonfire of inanities—the collection of paranoid whispers, the rebounding smears, the unsubstantiated allegations, the shifting stories, and the conflicting allegiances that coalesced to create the Russiagate panic, I want to provide more details on the previously mentioned use of foreign agents to create and dish out bogus allegations about members of the Trump team. It comes from a Cambridge University postgraduate student—and it involves the very same Stefan Halper, the operative with extensive ties to the CIA who took aim at Carter Page, Sam Clovis and, most infamously, George Papadopoulos.

In February 2014, Halper and his pals Richard Dearlove and Christopher Andrew, a Cambridge professor and an MI5 historian, were hosts of the Cambridge Intelligence Seminar, a gathering of former and current members of the intelligence community. During the event, they hosted a dinner that Lieutenant General Michael Flynn, then director of the Defense Intelligence Agency (DIA), attended with Dan O'Brien, a DIA official. Also present at the dinner was Svetlana Lokhova, a Russian-born academic who had studied with Christopher Andrew.

According to Lokhova, she talked briefly with Flynn. O'Brien told the *Wall Street Journal* that he didn't notice anything unusual about Lokhova and Flynn's interaction. And Lokhova's boyfriend, David North, says he picked her up—alone—after the dinner.[20]

Fast-forward to 2017, when this innocuous, inconsequential meeting became a flashpoint in the Russiagate narrative, resurfacing soon after Trump took office and appointed Flynn his national security advisor—and a leak revealed that Flynn had called the

Russian ambassador. Stories in the mainstream media recounted Flynn's "connection" to Lokhova. The subtext—no, actually, the main thrust of these stories—was that Lokhova was some kind of honeypot Russian spy who might have compromised Flynn. Where did this story come from?

Andrew kicked things off with an article in the *London Times* in February. From there, the story picked up steam with unnamed sources floating a Flynn-was-compromised storyline. Then in a May 2017 article, the *New York Times* reported on an unnamed FBI informant, who we now know was Halper—the same guy who tried entrap George Papadopoulos by actually luring him to London under the guise of a $3,000 payday—as the source of the rumor. Here, ladies and gentlemen, is how a bogus allegation begins to take a life of its own, shaping public opinion regardless of its veracity. Halper, the *Times* wrote, "was alarmed by the general's apparent closeness with a Russian woman who was also in attendance."[21] Incredible how Halper's sense of alarm seems to appear only around political opponents of the Obama administration (Flynn was a vocal opponent of Obama's signature foreign policy initiative, the Iran deal).

The *Times* continued: "The concern was strong enough that it prompted another person to pass on a warning to the American authorities that Mr. Flynn could be compromised by Russian intelligence, according to two people familiar with the matter."[22]

Frankly, this reporting raises more questions than it solves. Who exactly is "another person"? If Halper was an FBI informant, wouldn't he inform American authorities? Or, since Halper is based in England, was "another person" tied to MI6 or some other organization? The article doesn't say when Halper decided to voice his alarm. Was this back in 2014? Or was it more recent—say, around the time the FBI started to probe the Trump campaign and administration? That, in retrospect, seems far likelier.

The story behind the allegation is far more disturbing than the allegation itself, which is based purely on one brief public encounter. Without any further substantiation, it amounts to a hit job, an obvious smear, something that should never have even seen the light of day. Instead, I'm writing about it in a book!

"What Halper staged is a textbook 'black-op' to dirty up the reputation of a political opponent. He needed an innocuous social event to place Flynn in a room with a woman who was ethnically Russian. I was unlucky he picked me," said Lokhova, who filed a multimillion-dollar suit against Halper, the *Wall Street Journal*, and other media outlets in May 2019.[23]

There's more to this story—and we'll unfold it when we get to Plan B. But even without any additional shocking details, this fabricated allegation is important. It's yet another case of government agencies' using foreign operatives and far-flung events to create a confluence of swirling rumors around Trump and his team to incite paranoia and distrust.

"A" IS FOR ASPERSIONS

I could go on for days documenting the whirlpool of misinformation, innuendo, conflicts of interest, and foreign "intelligence" that has proven to be nothing more than stupidity. Peter Strzok, of all people, wasn't kidding when he said, "There's no big there there." Those five words summarize the hysteria around Russiagate as clearly as anything that's been said. That was Strzok's verdict before Mueller even took over. And you know what? That was Mueller's conclusion 675 days after he was appointed to investigate the collusion fantasy.

Why did it take so long? What the hell was going on here? Simply put, the faulty, warped, hostile, unsubstantiated aspersions that amassed into Plan A backfired. All the powerful ingredients of the plan—which had been gathered and consumed by senior members of the FBI, DOJ, and Robert Mueller's "dream team" of investigators—exploded.

Even without Glenn Simpson's calculated opposition "research" and plug-and-play plan, the conditions for this explosion had been gestating; restrictions on the ability for U.S. intelligence to share intel with foreign counterparts had been relaxed. A presidential candidate was rocking the long-established thinking regarding relations with Russia. When that candidate upset the heavily favored Democratic nominee, and reports surfaced of Russian attempts to influence and interfere in the election, the apparent optics of collusion gained unearned legitimacy in some quarters—especially among senior members of the Obama administration.

At the beginning of this chapter, I said Plan A didn't begin as a fully mapped-out strategy, but rather solidified into a war to smear Trump, emerging from the heavily politicized, power-crazed swamp that Washington has become. I still stand by that, although we may learn more as Attorney General William Barr investigates the origins of the FBI investigation.[24] But I want to include the muck manufacturing of foreign intelligence agencies, too. It turns out that the anti-Trump forces inside our intelligence community were using foreign spies to launder allegations—indeed, connections to two of America's "Five Eyes" brethren, Australia and England, have figured heavily in Russiagate. For example, the *Telegraph* reported on May 19, 2019, that British prime minister Theresa May's intelligence chiefs were briefed on Steele's information before Donald Trump was briefed,[25] and CNN reported back on April 14, 2017, that "British intelligence passed Trump associates communications with Russians on to U.S. counterparts."[26] When I think about the timeline and the double-talk from the likes of Brennan, Comey, Rosenstein, and others about what spurred the investigation—the dossier, Papadopoulos and Mifsud, or other "intelligence"—it's still hard to identify which communiqué or exchange was the pebble that turned Plan A into an avalanche of aspersions.

None of those aspersions have been proven true. But that didn't matter on July 31, 2016, as operation Crossfire Hurricane unfurled. Or three months later on October 31, when liberal editor David Corn delivered a Halloween horror story, reporting the uncorroborated allegations of the Steele dossier as if the "information" were legitimate. Or as Obama administration members began leaking sinister-sounding Russia-related stories about Michael Flynn and others on the Trump team. All of these tales, some beyond salacious and ridiculous, were repeated breathlessly by the anti-Trump mainstream media and retweeted and reposted. Papadopoulos didn't spread the virus that Mifsud apparently had planted on him, but the swamp's thirst for scandal and the media's thirst for clicks made sure it spread.

And the avalanche of aspersions worked. On May 17, 2017, acting Attorney General Rod Rosenstein appointed his old friend and colleague Robert Mueller as special counsel. His responsibility: to investigate "any links and/or coordination between the Russian government and individuals associated with the campaign of Donald Trump and any matters that arose or may arise from the investigation." If there was any doubt about the end game related to what Mueller was authorized to do, the appointment memo added some teeth: "The Special Counsel is authorized to prosecute Federal crimes arising from the investigation of these matters."[27]

Plan A was now complete. With the unleashing of the special counsel and his team of mad-dog Clinton-loving lawyers, the avalanche of aspersions would be thoroughly investigated. Trump and all his campaign team were now officially under assault.

CHAPTER 4

Plan B: The Road Map for Trashing the Trump Campaign

This is a chapter with a lot of moving parts. But those moving parts are crucial to explain how what I call Plan B emerged, what Plan B actually was, and why, ultimately, it was as flimsy as the paper the Steele dossier was printed on. But to avoid any confusion, let me summarize the plan right up front: while Christopher Steele was assembling his dossier for Glenn Simpson and Fusion GPS, he was also sending that same "intelligence" to the FBI. Footnotes in the FISA warrant applications provide the smoking gun on this. He was, as you will see, *double-dipping*—working for both the FBI and Glenn Simpson *at the same time.*

Initially, I believed that the Steele dossier was the FISA warrant application and the FISA warrant application was the Steele dossier. But I've now found evidence that indicates that, for reasons I'll get to in a second, Steele sent other reports to the FBI *detailing the same claims as in the dossier.* These reports fueled the FISA warrant applications, while the dossier fueled public outrage and served to destabilize Team Trump. Together, the Steele FBI reports and the Steele dossier became the inseparable damaging duo that was used to drive Russiagate forward and cast a paralyzing shadow on the Trump campaign and administration. Without the Steele dossier, there was no way to get the damaging allegations into the media and demand an investigation. Without the Steele reports to the FBI, there was no way to get a warrant approved. No warrant, no investigation. No investigation, no Mueller special counsel. No Mueller special counsel, no fabricated allegations of obstruction against the president.

The reason I'm making a distinction between the Steele dossier and the reports Steele sent to the FBI is that the FBI reports—which have never been seen by the public but are alluded to in multiple FISA warrant applications—are critical to providing cover for so many of the bad actors in this story. John Brennan repeatedly insisted that he first saw the dossier in December 2016, and Comey has repeatedly claimed ignorance regarding its provenance. This is possible. The dossier was only one aspect of Steele's anti-Trump intel campaign. By reporting to the FBI, verbally or otherwise, Steele was providing a method of plausible deniability for when officials would be asked if they had seen the dossier, *which was paid for by the Clinton Campaign and the DNC.* If this theory is correct—and the FISA warrant application says the FBI received reports from Steele, then Brennan didn't have to see the actual dossier because he could see the reports or summaries of the reports that Steele was providing to his intelligence connections through unofficial channels, while the FBI could also receive "reports" from Steele separate from the physical dossier.

Indeed, Peter Strzok, as head of FBI counterintelligence, reportedly briefed Brennan, so it is not a stretch to assume that he shared Steele's reports, which were not, technically, the dossier.[1] As for the FBI investigators, they could cop to the same story—"We never laid eyes on the dossier"—*because they didn't need the dossier when they were getting the same information directly from Steele.*

I lay out the proof of all this in subsequent pages. But here is the overarching takeaway: the Steele reports to the FBI—which mirrored the dossier—formed the basis of the FISA warrant application, and the FISA warrant application was based on the Steele reports to the FBI, which completely echo the dossier.

And all three of these things—the dossier, the Steele reports to the FBI, and the FISA warrant application—became the road map to the Mueller investigation. But I'm getting ahead of myself.

FUEL FOR A FIRE

According to official FBI lore, the formal investigation into Trump-Russia collusion kicked off July 31, 2016, with operation Crossfire Hurricane, the Strzok-led counterintelligence investigation. It was initiated, according to the FBI timeline, in response to Australian diplomat Alexander Downer's report claiming that George Papadopoulos had told him the Russians had some kind of damaging information on Hillary Clinton—something the former Trump advisor has consistently denied ever doing.

Somehow, when the *New York Times* published the first report of the Downer meeting on December 30, 2017, a huge piece of misinformation, attributed to "court documents," was slipped into the story: "In late April, at a London hotel, Mr. Mifsud told Mr. Papadopoulos that he had just learned from high-level Russian officials in Moscow that the Russians had 'dirt' on Mrs. Clinton in the form of 'thousands of emails,' according to court documents."

Two paragraphs later, the article reports: "Not long after, however, he opened up to Mr. Downer, the Australian diplomat, about his contacts with the Russians."[2]

In one article using anonymous sources and unspecified court documents—quite possibly the FISA warrant application regarding Carter Page, which mentions Papadopoulos on page eight and has a redacted footnote next to his name—two completely separate events are linked. But the fact is, Papadopoulos says he never specified that the Russians had Clinton's emails and, if anything, he was goaded into discussing Russia by Downer, who has now gone on record confirming Papadopoulos's assertion that emails were never mentioned. But the two events, presented without an ounce of skepticism in the article and evidently linked in court documents, became conflated.

So the source of the *Times*'s story seems to have known about the Mifsud meeting *and* the Downer meeting and merged the two events. Perhaps all this is in the Carter Page FISA warrant application—which I have reason to believe the *Times* reporters had seen. But if it isn't, find the person who spoon-fed this bombshell bogus storyline to "the Gray Lady" to establish an "official" investigation narrative, and you likely have identified one of the chief deep state architects of Russiagate.

A key figure in this inquiry is Bill Priestap, the assistant director of the FBI's Counterintelligence Division, who supervised Strzok. Thanks to one of Strzok's texts, we now know that on or around May 9, 2016—about two weeks after Papadopoulos's April 26 meeting with Mifsud and just days after Papadopoulos's May 1 meeting with Downer—Priestap traveled to London (amazing how many times London surfaces in Russiagate, isn't it?). In a May 4, 2016, text to Lisa Page, Strzok wonders about Priestap's ability to read a memo "before he gets back from London next week." Then on May 9, Strzok sent a text wondering who would get a briefing "with Bill out."[3]

What was the point of the London trip? According to testimony Priestap gave to Congress in a closed-door meeting on June 5, 2018, he "went to meet with a foreign partner, a foreign government partner." Priestap refused to specify whom this foreign partner was or whether his trip had anything to do with the Trump-Russia investigation.[4]

It seems more than likely that a senior FBI counterintelligence director would go to London to meet members of British intelligence, doesn't it?

Remember: Papadopoulos, the young Trump advisor, was popping up everywhere. The *Washington Post* had written about him. The Israeli press had covered him. And he was the victim of a sensational-ized front-page news hit by the *Times* of London on May 4. Moreover, Papadopoulos lived in London for months in 2016. He worked for a nebulous law institute whose staff included a British woman who had worked, on occasion, with the FBI—which, according to Papadopoulos, tried to ensure that Mifsud would meet him in Rome.

Still, the whole manufactured storyline regarding Papadopoulos—who North Carolina congressman Mark Meadows said was "the whole reason we have this Russian collusion investigation going on"[5] was prob-lematic in terms of taking down Trump and his team.

That's because Papadopoulos never mentioned the Clinton-email angle to Downer and wisely never repeated Mifsud's "Russia has Clin-ton's emails" claims to anyone on the campaign team. And those two facts really put the kibosh on any plan to plant or prove a collusion storyline. In other words, two key parts of the Russiagate fantasy, as far as roping in Papadopoulos is concerned, cannot be proven *because they never happened.*

And that means the investigation into Papadopoulos was destined to fail as far as hurting or tainting Trump. As we know from his book, Papadopoulos was threatened with FARA charges unless he pleaded to the much lesser charge of lying to the FBI, which he did.[6] So the Mueller investigation basically wound up going from sixty to zero with Papadopoulos.

If Papadopoulos was going to be a bust, FBI agents needed to broaden the scope of the investigation and ensnarl other members of the Trump team. To do that, they needed a FISA warrant.

Why was a FISA warrant needed?

According to Section 702 of the FISA, U.S. law enforcement and intelligence agencies can spy on any and every non-U.S. citizen if an investigation hinges on "national security." If, however, American communications are swept up during an investigation, that information is supposed to be "minimized" and remain unseen, in compliance with Fourth Amendment protections against unlawful search and seizure regarding U.S. citizens. This means that any surveillance of an American suspected of working as or with a foreign agent requires a warrant.[7]

Since Trump's campaign was populated, obviously, by Americans, any probe investigating so-called collusion with Russia required a FISA warrant.

THE FICTION OF FUSION

Enter the plug-and-play work of Glenn Simpson, Fusion GPS, Christopher Steele, and ultimately the Steele dossier, which served at least four functions for the deep state operatives in the Obama administration.

First, it became a compendium—a virtual scandal-a-day diary—of allegations and fantasies about Trump and his campaign that could be weaponized.

Second, it provided a way to "legitimize" the previous reports from foreign intelligence agencies that could not be used against U.S. citizens. Steele, who had been a paid operative for the FBI, was a known and therefore credible source, which was a requirement of the Woods verification procedures that were part of FISA application protocol.

Third, it turns out Steele wasn't just a former informant for the FBI. The footnotes in the FISA warrant application reveal he was actively working with the FBI while he was collecting information for the dossier.[8]

Fourth, and most important, it provided Steele with the allegations he would relay to the FBI. Not only did this allow the bureau to build a road map to obtain the FISA warrant by citing Steele as a reliable source, but Steele's information also provided a road map for the entire Mueller investigation as well.

The Steele dossier mentions very few members of the Trump campaign, and almost all of them—Papadopoulos, Flynn, Manafort, Stone—have been indicted. Ironically, Carter Page, the man the FISA warrant focused on, has had his name dragged through the mud but has never been charged with anything. It's also ironic that all the charges for Papadopoulos, Flynn, and Manafort have *nothing* to do with the dossier or Russiagate. The indictments, just to be crystal clear, involve lying to the FBI, FARA law issues, money laundering, and tax evasion.

Timing in love, real estate, and war is always important. The same goes for politics and prosecutions. Now that the optics of a collusion storyline had been planted—thanks to the presence of Paul Manafort, to Trump's stump-speech quotes about Russia, to Carter Page's ties to Russia, and to unspecified reports from foreign agents—the FBI thought it had the goods for the usually rubber-stamping FISA court.

In the summer, the FBI applied to the FISA court for a warrant "to monitor four members of the Trump team suspected of irregular contacts with Russian officials," according to the *Guardian*.[9]

A FISA warrant on any member of the campaign would allow open-season surveillance on the entire Trump team because the warrant allows the invocation of the "two-hop" rule. That is, any Americans the suspect talks to can be investigated, and their contacts listened to as well.

But the initial FISA request was denied. The *Guardian* reported that the application was turned down and that the FISA court asked the "FBI counter-intelligence investigators to narrow its focus."[10]

Evidently, the court found the application too broad, which is somewhat shocking because FISA applications in the age of post-9/11 terror have a rubber-stamp reputation—very few are rejected. One published report found that the court has rejected eleven applications and approved 33,942 since its creation.[11] The rejection meant the bureau needed to bolster its application. It needed to make the case that spying on Carter Page and the Trump campaign was a serious national security issue. It needed to document widespread, sinister events. But how?

The bureau needed more intel, and fast. The election was now four months away. And if Trump had defied the predictions of political insiders to win the Republican nomination, who was to say he wouldn't do the same thing against a problematic candidate like Hillary Clinton? Time was of the essence.

Glenn Simpson had already hired Nellie Ohr. He had already met with Bruce Ohr. He had even reached out to Christopher Steele, the FBI-approved informant and former spymaster. And he had nabbed a $2 million payday from the legal team working for the DNC and the Clinton campaign.

There was just one problem. One of the FBI's intel-collection sources—and possibly one of Glenn Simpson's sources—had dried up.

AN ILLEGAL COLLECTION AGENCY

That source was likely the enormous database of digital communications maintained by the NSA. Using the powers granted in FISA's Section 702, the NSA conducts massive data sweeps of internet communications on a regular basis. There are two primary methods: upstream surveillance, which, according to the Electronic Frontier Foundation, involves collecting communications as they travel through internet backbone carriers—that is, the system's largest top-tier data routes and connectors—and downstream surveillance, also called PRISM, which gathers communications from companies like Google, Facebook, and Yahoo![12]

Law enforcement and intel agencies with clearance can query these databases, requesting communications that are from or to foreign intelligence targets. These search parameters—or "selectors"—can include specific email addresses or phone numbers but can be much broader. If the search is conducted under the guise of a "vital national security" issue, results containing data from Americans can be opened and all "upstream" connections explored.

As long as the people making the queries strictly abide by constitutional provisions and there are supervisors prepared to conduct due diligence to ensure the searches are not being abused, this kind of surveillance makes sense, especially in a post-9/11 world. But there must be checks and balances. You want to investigate an American citizen and conduct surveillance? Get. A. Warrant.

That is the law of the land.

We now know, however, that this wasn't always the case. Contractors working on behalf of government organizations were also querying the NSA database. According to an April 26, 2017, FISA Memorandum Opinion and Order, numerous queries were being conducted by the intelligence community as well as by or on behalf of contractors and individuals without proper authorization. These searches revealed information about U.S. citizens and were not clearly related to national security. Therefore, making these queries and viewing the result sets should have required FISA court approval.[13]

Furthermore, according to the FISA Court order,

"[o]n March 9, 2016, DOJ oversight personnel conducting a minimization review at the FBI's [redacted] learned that the FBI had disclosed raw FISA information, including but not limited to Section 702-acquired information....[redacted] is part of the [redacted] and 'is largely staffed by private contractors'.... certain [redacted] contractors had access to raw FISA information on FBI storage systems" that "went well beyond what was necessary to respond to the FBI's requests.... The FBI discontinued the above-described access to raw FISA information as of April 18, 2016." [14]

According to the memorandum, the consultants were used to "provide technical or linguistic assistance to the FBI." But there are a couple of interesting things about these revelations. First, the timing: in March 2016, just as George Papadopoulos was joining the campaign team, the DOJ discovered potential violations. Then it took five more weeks for the query capability to be shut down. Second, the idea that these illegal queries were in conjunction with translators and tech experts raises questions, too. Who were those translators? And did any of them have connections to the people and companies paid to gather dirt on the Trump team?

Whatever the answer, the fact remains that the FBI was playing fast and loose with FISA data related to American citizens. But as of April 26, the rules of the game—no spying on Americans—were now being enforced and tracked. In fact, some noncompliance reports reached NSA director Mike Rogers, and he was clearly not comfortable with what he was hearing and reading, because he ordered a full audit on Section 702 compliance in mid-June 2016.[15]

So between operation Crossfire Hurricane's falling apart as the Papadopoulos "lead" evaporated and a clampdown on collecting info on Team Trump in normal intelligence sweeps (the phone calls, the emails, the text contacts), investigating collusion concerns was not going to be a walk in the park. And using intel that had been illegally gathered was never going to make it in court, either. The FBI needed sanitized intelligence.

AN INTEL CLEARINGHOUSE

Luckily for the bureau—and unluckily for Trump and America—Glenn Simpson's team appears to have figured out a way to launder specious secondhand and thirdhand allegations into alarming "raw intelligence."

What is "raw intelligence"? It's one of the building blocks of spycraft. The FBI, on its own website, says: "Simply defined, intelligence is information relevant to decision-making."[16] Raw intelligence, then, is data that has not been analyzed and evaluated.

By hiring Christopher Steele, a former MI6 Russian expert, Simpson effectively figured out a way to create a kind of magical quote machine to pump out shocking, scandalous data—essentially damning rumors that sounded like they could maybe, somehow, in some alternate universe be true. Remember that Simpson's wife actually bragged about this on Facebook, posting that her husband was the one who had driven the dossier. And that may be true. But Simpson needed Steele, or someone with Steele's reputation, as a Russian intel expert.

For most of the bigwigs at the FBI and Department of Justice, the British spy's résumé made him an unimpeachable delivery system for unsubstantiated data to be fed to Washington law enforcement and drive a paranoid collusion narrative that would wound and possibly kill the Trump campaign. I say "most of," because evidence now reveals that some members of the DOJ had "continued concerns" about the FISA warrant application, specifically about a confidential source cited in the document.

Once again, this information comes to us via the texts of Lisa Page, the FBI lawyer eventually dismissed from the Mueller special counsel team. In one message, she appears confident that the bureau can explain away any suggestion of bias—presumably the fact that Christopher Steele, who was employed by Glenn Simpson, who was employed by Hillary Clinton and the Democratic National Committee, might not be the most even-handed source. She also notes that Stuart Evans, then the DOJ's National Security Division deputy assistant attorney general, had repeatedly taken issue with the application:

"OI [Office of Intelligence] now has a robust explanation re any possible bias of the CHS [confidential human source] in the package," Page wrote to Andrew McCabe on October 12, 2016. "Don't know what the holdup is now, other than Stu's continued concerns."[17]

There was also at least one other person who raised flags to FBI investigators about the veracity and slant of Steele's information and the possible bias of Christopher Steele himself: Bruce Ohr, the DOJ's deputy attorney general, whose own wife worked for Glenn Simpson.

We now know that while she was employed by Simpson, Nellie Ohr fed her husband and other DOJ prosecutors anti-Trump reports during the 2016 campaign. Hidden in 339 pages of Bruce Ohr's communications that were released by the DOJ were "Hi Honey" emails from Nellie to her husband that shared her research tracking corruption in Russia and Ukraine.

"Ohr sent reams of open-source intelligence to her husband, Associate Deputy Attorney General Bruce Ohr, and on some occasions to at least three DOJ prosecutors: Lisa Holtyn, Ivana Nizich and Joseph Wheatley," as John Solomon reported for *The Hill*, noting that she sent "intelligence affecting Russian figures she told Congress she had tried to connect to Trump or Manafort."[18]

"Hi Honey, if you ever get a moment you might find the penultimate article interesting—especially the summary in the final paragraph," Nellie Ohr emailed her husband on July 6, 2016, in one typical communication. The article and paragraph she flagged suggested that Trump was a Putin stooge: "**If Putin wanted to concoct the ideal candidate to service his purposes, his laboratory creation would look like Donald Trump.**"[19]

The Fusion GPS researcher bolded that last sentence apparently for emphasis.

Ohr's emails represent another way that Brennan, Clapper, and the FBI could have seen so-called intelligence that helped stoke the collusion narrative without relying on the dossier. Did Nellie Ohr's tips get forwarded around D.C.? It seems entirely possible and entirely probable, given the Never Trump movement that was growing in the swamp.

Bruce Ohr testified on Tuesday, August 28, 2018, before the House Judiciary Committee that he had repeatedly warned FBI investigators—and Mueller's investigative bulldog Andrew Weissmann, who was at the DOJ at the time—that Christopher Steele had been "desperate that Trump not be elected." Ohr drew this conclusion after Steele reached out to him and arranged for them to meet on July 30, 2016, at the Mayflower Hotel in Washington, D.C. The meeting was also attended by Ohr's wife, Nellie.[20]

One day after that meeting, Bruce Ohr contacted members of the FBI and cautioned them when it came to evaluating Steele's reports. "I provided information to the FBI when I thought Christopher Steele was, as I said, desperate that Trump not be elected."

Ohr testified that he reached out to his bureau connections "[i]n case there might be any kind of bias or anything like that." He said he warned the FBI about the quality of the intel: "I don't know how reliable it is. You're going to have to check it out and be aware."

The transcript reveals that Ohr also told FBI agents that his wife and Steele were both working for Fusion GPS—and spelled out connections between the research group and Clinton. Here's a critical exchange between then South Carolina representative Trey Gowdy and Ohr:

> *Mr. Gowdy. So you specifically told the Bureau that the information you were passing on came from someone who was employed by the DNC, albeit in a somewhat triangulated way?*
>
> *Mr. Ohr. I don't believe I used—I didn't know they were employed by the DNC, but I certainly said, yes, that—that they were working for—you know, they were somehow working associated with the Clinton campaign. And I also told the FBI that my wife worked for Fusion GPS or was a contractor for GPS, Fusion GPS.*[21]

"I certainly told the FBI that Fusion GPS was working with—doing opposition research on Donald Trump," Ohr told congressional investigators, adding that he warned the FBI that Steele had expressed bias during their conversations. "I provided information to the FBI when I thought Christopher Steele was, as I said, desperate that Trump not be elected. So, yes, of course I provided that to the FBI.

"These guys were hired by somebody relating to—who's related to the Clinton campaign," Ohr said, admonishing the FBI to "be aware."

Until Simpson and Steele come clean on their working methods and sources—were sources incentivized to come up with explosive allegations?—the raw intelligence they provided should be regarded as illegitimate. Seriously, it belongs in an intel decontamination lab. Did

Simpson feed Steele sources and quotes? And if so, did Steele vet what he was given or just take everything as gospel from his boss? These would be natural questions for any investigation.

But because of Steele's reputation and his previous experience working on a headline-grabbing international soccer scandal with the FBI, bureau investigators and the FISA court bought the raw intel as legit—or at least worthy of evaluation.

Even if it was unfounded paranoia- and perversion-fueled gossip, it wound up being taken seriously. Seriously enough that it formed the bedrock of the most corrupt counterintelligence investigation in U.S. history.

Steele was hired before the initial FISA rejection. So he was ready to go in his hour of need. The first Steele memo was dated June 20, 2016."[22] As noted earlier, it was numbered 080, which suggests there were other memos—presumably a 079, a 078, or maybe even a 001 memo. But let's not get sidetracked by missing memos. The fact is that 080 is a big opening shot.

Here's what it claims:

1. **Russia had been "cultivating and supporting" Trump for "at least 5 years."**
2. **The Trump operation was directed by Putin, whose ultimate goal was to sow disunity in the U.S. and within the Transatlantic Alliance.**
3. **The Kremlin had been feeding Trump damaging intel on "democratic rivals."**
4. **The Kremlin had offered Trump "various lucrative real estate development and business deals in Russia.… However, so far, for reasons unknown, Trump had not taken any of these."**
5. **Russia had a file of *kompromat* on Hillary Clinton that was controlled by Putin spokesman Dmitry Peskov.**
6. **A trove of compromising material—sexual in nature—had been obtained by Russia to blackmail Trump.**[23]

Two hundred ninety days elapsed between the start of operation Crossfire Hurricane and the start of the Mueller investigation. Then 674 days passed before Mueller submitted his report. In those 964 days, guess how many of the claims in the dossier's first memo were proven beyond a reasonable doubt?

None. Zero. Zip. *Nada.*

Look, I'm willing to concede that portions of #2 above have some basis in reality. Trump's own advisors believe Russia tried to interfere in the election. This is what Russia and other foreign governments do. And there is no doubt that Russia and Russian agents conducted social media-influencing campaigns. So I get it. There is substantial evidence that the Kremlin played dirty, and Putin doesn't like being subservient to the West, which Russia relies on for cash and imports. But the cyber-charges were broad and lacked any original detail. Remember, more than one month before WikiLeaks published the hacked DNC emails, WikiLeaks mastermind Julian Assange told the world he had damaging material! "We have upcoming leaks in relation to Hillary Clinton," he said to British television network ITV on June 12, 2016—eight days before the first dossier memo. "We have emails pending publication."[24]

In other words, I could have written similar Russian cyberinterference memos at home on my couch and been as factually correct as the dossier. Or, to put it another way, when it came to dossier memo 080, there was, as Trump-hater Strzok once worried, "no big there there."

The third charge in the dossier, of feeding "damaging intel," is also unsubstantiated. The only identified approach to the Trump campaign with damaging intel came at the Trump Tower meeting, from Natalia Veselnitskaya, a woman working with Fusion GPS who delivered nothing of any consequence. The "intel," if you can even call it that, was about her objections to the Magnitsky Act and had nothing to do with Hillary Clinton's emails or anyone else's.

As for the alleged real estate deals, this is absurd. Trump didn't take any deals, per the memo. So what is the problem? I'm sure some people now believe that lawyer Michael Cohen's congressional testimony stating he been working on a deal for a Trump Tower in Moscow during the campaign somehow corroborates this charge. He even said he was pushing the deal as late as June 2016. Still, consider the source. Cohen's testimony itself is dubious because he was facing a long stint in the big house. Furthermore, as Trump himself has noted, he was a businessman engaged in an uncertain campaign. He was conducting business internationally, as he had for decades. Finally, there was no deal. True to his word, Trump made no deal.

As for the January 2016 email Cohen wrote that was "addressed" to Russian president Vladimir Putin's spokesman Dmitry Peskov asking for help on the Trump Tower Moscow project, the charge is ridiculous. Sure, Cohen wrote the email, but it was a shot in the dark—he didn't have Peskov's email address! Here's how the Trump-hating *New York Times* described it: "But Mr. Cohen did not appear to have Mr. Peskov's direct email, and instead wrote to a general inbox for press inquiries."[25] So why was this even an issue? It was just another bogus, hyped-up storyline. And when it came time to press charges against Cohen, Mueller left out clarifying information to make it seem like this real estate deal was much higher-level and more suspicious than it was.

At any rate, it is possible that Mueller and the Collusion Chorus consider Cohen's email as evidence vindicating the real estate allegations in the Steele dossier. If that's the case, that just supports the idea that Mueller was using the dossier as a justification for endlessly investigating Trump as well as to salvage the broken reputations of the DOJ and FBI for relying on Steele's information. If Mueller could show something, anything, in the dossier and if Steele's information had a sliver of truth, then he could vindicate the FBI and DOJ.

Let's go on to the second memo in the dossier, 086, dated July 26, 2016. This focuses largely on Russia's cyberinfluencing, espionage, and hacking. Again, of all the dossier dishing, this has proved to be the most compelling. But let's consider the historical context of this memo. On July 22, 2016, WikiLeaks published a huge trove of hacked emails from the Democratic National Committee. It was a stunning, damning, embarrassing dump. *Four* days later, Christopher Steele reported that one month earlier, he had been told that Russia prioritizes "state-sponsored" attacks against Western governments. Anyone think the timing and subject matter here might be suspect? It seems clear that Steele provided intelligence to suggest that Russia might be behind the recent hacking.

And guess what? The next memo laid out in the dossier, 095, doesn't have a date on it but it confirms that Russia was behind the DNC hack. Here are two notable allegations:

- "An ethnic Russian close associate of Republican Presidential Candidate Donald Trump" said there was a "conspiracy of cooperation" between Trump and Russian leadership, and that it was "managed" by Paul Manafort, Carter Page, "and others."
- The same source said the Russian regime was behind the email hacking of the DNC and that the Trump team had been aware of the operation. "In return the Trump team had agreed to sideline Russian intervention in Ukraine" as a campaign and NATO issue.[26]

The reason the above dossier tidbits are so interesting and horrifying is that we now know the identity of Source E, who not only made these charges but also provided salacious charges about Trump and prostitutes. Sergei Millian was the apparently unwitting man listed as Sources D and E, according to the *Wall Street Journal*, who spilled his tales to an associate, who then passed them on to Steele.[27] The dossier calls him "an ethnic Russian close associate of Republican Presidential Candidate Donald Trump." Based on everything we know about Millian—who did not respond to the paper's asking him if he was a source for the dossier— the description of him as a "close associate" of Trump is laughable. Did Millian, who apparently exchanged emails with Michael Cohen, try to pump up his own reputation when talking to Steele's source? Or did Steele's source pump up Millian's connection to Trump? Or did Steele?

All these unanswered questions and so much uncertainty show how suspect raw intelligence—especially Steele's raw intelligence—can be.

Seriously, the only thing that has been 100 percent verified in the entire Steele dossier is the claim that Carter Page did, in fact, travel to Russia, which isn't novel and certainly is not a crime. I've traveled to Russia twice; is there a dossier on me, too? Maybe a FISA warrant?

How did investigators separate the fact from the fantasy?

It appears that until they had the FISA warrant in hand, they didn't want to.

A BOMBSHELL IN THE FOOTNOTES

Here is the thing about the FBI's Russiagate FISA warrant applications: the details about Steele subtly change over time. And they reveal that Steele reported his "raw intelligence"—that is, lies—directly to the FBI.

Look at what the FBI wrote on pages fifteen and sixteen of the FISA warrant application of October 2016. Keep in mind that "Source #1" is clearly Christopher Steele, "U.S. person" is clearly Glenn Simpson, "U.S.-based law firm" is clearly Perkins Coie, and "Candidate #1" is clearly Donald Trump:

> *Source #1 [redacted] and has been an FBI source since [redacted]. Source #1's reporting has been corroborated and used in criminal proceedings and the FBI assesses Source #1 to be reliable. **Source #1 has been compensated [redacted] by the FBI** [emphasis mine] and the FBI is unaware of any derogatory information pertaining to Source #1.*
>
> *Source #1, who now owns a foreign business/financial intelligence firm, was approached by an identified U.S. person, who indicated to Source #1 **that a U.S.-based law firm had hired the identified U.S. person to conduct research regarding Candidate #1's ties to Russia** [emphasis mine] (the identified U.S. person and Source #1 have a long-standing business relationship). The identified U.S. person hired Source*

#1 to conduct this research. The identified U.S. person never advised the motivation behind the research into Candidate #1's ties to Russia. The FBI speculates that the identified U.S. person was likely looking for information that could be used to discredit Candidate #1's campaign.

Source #1 tasked his sub-source(s) to collect the requisite information. After Source #1 received information from the sub-source(s), described herein, **Source #1 provided the information to the identified U.S. person who had hired Source #1 and to the FBI** *[emphasis mine].* *[Redacted]*

Notwithstanding Source #1's reason for conducting the research into Candidate #1's ties to Russia, based on Source #1's previous reporting history with the FBI, whereby Source #1 provided reliable information to the FBI, the FBI believes Source #1's reporting herein to be credible.[28]

The key takeaways here, which I bolded above, are that the FBI never stated that the DNC and the Clinton campaign were paying Simpson and Steele via Perkins Coie; that the FBI was paying Steele for the information used in the application; and—this is the killer revelation—that the information he provided the FBI was *the same information that was in the dossier he compiled for Simpson's Fusion GPS and their clients Clinton and the DNC.*

This is right there in black and white: Steele was filing two sets of documents. One was the dossier—which was fed to the media (and presumably the DNC and the Clinton campaign). The other set of reports went to the FBI. They may have been the same exact reports for all we know. But to maintain plausible deniability and promote the myth that there was some separate "other" intelligence source that Clapper, Brennan, and the FBI had seen, the Steele reports to the FBI were never referred to as "the dossier." FBI agents didn't mention that particular document because Steele was funneling them separate reports—*of the same dirt!*

Eight pages later, the application discusses journalist Michael Isikoff's September 23, 2016, story titled "U.S. intel officials probe ties between Trump adviser and Kremlin."[29]

In the article, Isikoff reports that Carter Page is being investigated to determine if he opened up "communications with senior Russian officials" to discuss "the possible lifting of economic sanctions if the Republican nominee becomes president." The story cites multiple sources, but the October FISA warrant application, as I'm about to show, tries to clear Steele of driving the September 23rd "news" article. Somehow, though, the application authors failed to note that Isikoff is friends[30] with Glenn Simpson, the "business associate" in this application footnote. Here:

> As discussed above, Source #1 was hired by a business associate to conduct research into Candidate #1's ties to Russia. Source #1 provided the results of his research to the business associate, and the FBI assesses that the business associate likely provided this information to the law firm that hired the business associate in the first place. Source #1 told the FBI that he/she only provided this information to the business associate and the FBI. [redacted]
>
> The FBI does not believe that Source #1 directly provided this information to the identified news organization that published the September 23rd News Article.[31]

When it came time to update the FISA warrant in January 2017—because, as noted previously, the warrants are issued only for ninety-day terms—Steele's relationship with the FBI had changed. The bureau told the court that it had "suspended its relationship" with Steele because of an "unauthorized disclosure" to the press—the leaked dossier. But the agency insisted this politicized behavior didn't discredit the previous information it received. Here it is on page seventeen of the January FISA warrant application:

> Source #1 has been an FBI source since [redacted]. Source #1 has been compensated [redacted] by the FBI. [Redacted]
>
> ...in or about October 2016, the FBI suspended its relationship with Source #1 due to Source #1's unauthorized disclosure of information to the press. Notwithstanding the suspension of its relationship with Source

#1, the FBI assesses Source #1 to be reliable as previous reporting from Source #1 has been corroborated and used in criminal proceedings. Moreover, the FBI notes that the incident that led to the FBI suspending its relationship with Source #1 occurred after Source #1 provided the reporting that is described herein.

Source who now owns a foreign business/financial intelligence firm, was approached by an identified US. person, who indicated to Source #1 that a U.S.-based law firm had hired the identified US. person to conduct research regarding Candidate #1's ties to Russia (the identified US. person and Source #1 have a long-standing business relationship). The identified US. person hired Source #1 to conduct this research. The identified US. person never advised Source #1 as to the motivation behind the research into Candidate #1's ties to Russia. The FBI speculates that the identified US. person was likely looking for information that could be used to discredit Candidate #1's campaign.[32]

But then the application gets really revelatory about why Steele went public with his dossier. Here:

...in or about late October 2016, however, after the Director of the FBI sent a letter to the US. Congress, which stated that the FBI had learned of new information that might be pertinent to an investigation that the FBI was conducting of Candidate #2. Source #1 told the FBI that he/she was frustrated with this action and believed it would likely influence the 2016 US. [sic] Presidential 1 election. In response to Source #1's concerns, Source #1 independently, and against the prior admonishment from the FBI to speak only with the FBI on this matter, released the reporting discussed herein to an identified news organization. Although the FBI continues to assess Source #1's reporting is reliable, as noted above, the FBI has suspended its relationship with Source #1 because of this disclosure.[33]

There it is, in black and white! Steele pushed the dossier on the public because he was mad that James Comey had reopened the email investigation on Trump rival Hillary Clinton just eight days before the election. He actually told the FBI he was afraid Donald Trump was going to win.

And despite his overt, obvious bias, the FBI still refused to discount his reports. Instead, it continued to double down on his garbage reports. It doubled down on a double-dipping, anti-Trump source who may have been spun by double-agent informants, for all anyone knows.

In April 2017, Comey once again signed off on the second FISA warrant renewal. This time, footnote ten on pages seventeen and eighteen reveals that Steele had been fired:

> *[I]n or about October 2016, the FBI suspended its relationship with Source #1 due to Source #1's unauthorized disclosure of information to the press. Subsequently, the FBI closed Source #1 as an FBI source. Nevertheless, the FBI assesses Source #1 to be reliable as previous reporting from Source #1 has been corroborated and used in criminal proceedings. Moreover, the FBI notes that the incident that led the FBI to terminate its relationship with Source #1 occurred after Source #1 provided the reporting that is described herein.*[34]

In other words, the FBI claims that despite Steele's indiscretion, despite his inability to follow directions from his handlers, despite his clear-cut distress over the idea that Trump might win an election, despite his apparent anger at the timing of James Comey's announcement regarding the reopening of the Clinton email investigation, and despite the fact the FBI suspended, and then ended, its relationship with its primary source, all the information that Christopher "Source #1" Steele provided to the FBI on Russiagate was still deemed worthy.

Is anyone surprised the FBI would say that? And that Comey would sign off on that multiple times? The bureau needed those reports because *that's all it had!*

Luckily for the FBI, the FISA Court kept buying what it was selling.

And once the FBI had the FISA warrant, it was open season on Team Trump and the Trump presidency, given that the final two FISA warrant renewals happened when Trump was firmly established in office. The "two-hop" rule could ensnare most of the Trump operation. Agents could access email. They could interview suspects and the associates, friends, and family of suspects. And if people didn't want to talk, the FBI could issue subpoenas forcing them to testify in front of grand juries.

With all this, the FBI could and did amass mountains of information. They could then quiz suspects like Papadopoulos. And if a date or detail was misstated or inaccurately recalled?

They could hit 'em with a federal crime charge: lying—whether the person meant to or not—to an FBI agent.

BACK TO THE FUTURE

Now that we've established the irrefutably shoddy nature of Christopher Steele's dossier and his reports to the FBI, and how vital it was for the bureau to use his "intelligence" to obtain a FISA warrant in order to put the Trump campaign and administration under a legal microscope, we need to go back in time to examine what would normally be truly uncanny connections to the past.

But since these connections appear to have Glenn Simpson's fingerprints on them, perhaps it's not uncanny at all. Perhaps it is all of a piece.

If Steele's reports begat the FISA warrant, then Glenn Simpson's 2007 article in the *Wall Street Journal* begat Steele's reports.

Yes, the article is largely about big-name Washingtonians lobbying on behalf of ex-Soviet billionaires—most notably about Republican stalwart Bob Dole's being paid to help a Russian oligarch and about former FBI director William Sessions's representing a Russian mobster. But an examination of the story reveals a familiar cast of characters.[35] Dole had been contacted by Paul Manafort, who had been an advisor on Dole's presidential campaign. Manafort was working for Oleg Deripaska. Deripaska was and still is reputed to be one of Vladimir Putin's closest associates. The article also mentions Manafort's working for Ukrainian prime minister Viktor Yanukovych, another Manafort client. Guess what? Yanukovych wound up with multiple mentions in the Steele dossier as well, mostly in dispatches about how Manafort had received sizable kickbacks from him, which had been reported elsewhere in the media.

The subsequent story by Sara Carter in *Circa* that I cited in the first chapter spells out even more connections.[36] Putin, upset by Deripaska's visa troubles, deployed Russian deputy foreign minister Sergey Kislyak to lobby U.S. ambassador to Moscow William Burns to try to solve Deripaska's U.S. visa problems. Putin eventually dispatched Kislyak to be his ambassador in Washington, where he got sucked into Russiagate for his contacts with Jeff Sessions. Ironically, Sessions's failure to recall meeting with Kislyak—a brief, public encounter—is one of the reasons he recused himself from overseeing the Department of Justice's inquiry into the Trump-Russia fantasy.

You can't make this stuff up.

But let's stick to Manafort and Deripaska. Glenn Simpson's article reveals that he knew a good deal about both men as well as Yanukovych. As I noted earlier, this is the article in which he basically accuses Manafort of being an unregistered foreign agent with this line: "Mr. Manafort, who isn't registered as a consultant to the Ukrainian leader, didn't respond to requests for comment."[37]

As it happens, Manafort and Deripaska also figured in a previous presidential campaign—and it raised flags for intelligence officers. I covered some of this earlier, but now, in the context of the Steele dossier, you can really see the plug-and-play in action.

Here's what Simpson must have known: that Manafort's pal and colleague Rick Davis had run John McCain's campaign; that Davis, like Manafort, was in deep with the Russians, despite McCain's growing distrust of the Putin regime; and that a significant sector of the McCain campaign considered Davis and his Eastern Europe connections toxic and hypocritical.

Here's what Jeffrey H. Birnbaum and John Solomon wrote in a 2008 *Washington Post* story:

> *Within the campaign, Davis's role has been controversial from the*
> *start, as some aides in late 2006 argued to McCain that the Davis firm's*
> *work overseas conflicted with the senator's record as a pro-democracy*
> *champion and an advocate of reducing the influence of lobbyists in*
> *Washington, according to two people familiar with the conversations.*
> *The sources spoke on the condition of anonymity because of the sensitivity*
> *of internal campaign conversations. The aides questioned whether Davis*
> *should be given an important title in the campaign because that would*
> *make him more vulnerable to criticism, the sources said.*[38]

So Simpson likely knew that Manafort's partner had been a divisive figure. And he had good reason to suspect that Manafort, with his well-known track record of running interference with a number of African strongmen,[39] including kleptocrat Ferdinand Marcos of the Philippines and brutal Indonesian president Suharto, would be a divisive figure on team Trump. And if he wasn't a problem within the campaign (although it turned out that he was; Corey Lewandowski, whom Manafort supplanted, did not go quietly), Manafort would make an easy target for Trump's opposition.

It turns out that Manafort did try to join the McCain team, but his reputation raised flags, according to John Weaver, one of McCain's top campaign advisors at the time. Here's Sara Carter's description:

> *"Davis repeatedly tried to bring Manafort into the McCain campaign*
> *and we were able to stop it and even have Davis removed for his ties*
> *to pro-Russian efforts," Weaver said. "But this was short-lived as Davis*
> *actually and literally cried to the Senator every day for weeks until John*
> *relented and allowed Davis back."*[40]

If Simpson knew that Manafort's efforts to join the McCain campaign had caused a backlash, well, all the better—from his point of view. If McCain loyalists thought Manafort was tainted, no doubt law enforcement agents might want to investigate him. Remember, intelligence operatives did warn McCain. As the *Circa* article reports:

McCain's office also was warned by U.S. intelligence about possible Russian military connections to one of his policy advisers at the IRI [International Republican Institute], causing aides to scramble to separate the Russian-born expert from the U.S. senator, U.S. officials and McCain aides said.[41]

This last fact is explosive, hypocritical, and vital to the manufacture of the Russiagate scandal. One presidential candidate—John McCain—was warned about the Russian connections and possible influencing operations that ran counter to U.S. policy. U.S. intelligence operatives working for the Republican Bush administration warned him. Another presidential candidate, Donald Trump, running for election while the Democratic Obama administration was in power, *wasn't* warned about a guy with an even more controversial past and suspect connections—and who was also the partner of the guy whom McCain was warned about.

Did someone just drop the ball? Or was there a double standard, and corrupt Obama administration officials wanted to see Trump's campaign tainted by a criminal element?

When Manafort talked his way onto the Trump team, Glenn Simpson knew all of this. This is his plug-and-play miracle. Now there was a red-flag operative within the Trump campaign. He could leak everything he knew about Manafort. He could channel it, which he evidently did, to his hired gun, Christopher Steele. Together, he and Steele could dish their Manafort dirt to the FBI and watch a crippling investigation play out.

But here's the thing: just because Manafort was tainted doesn't mean that the entire Trump team was—and, most important, it doesn't mean Trump was.

So Glenn Simpson and Chris Steele went to town. They found "sources" to make explosive, frightening, mind-blowing charges. They used Russian disinformation specialists Trubnikov and Surkov. They located a source—Sergei Millian, according to the *Washington*

Post—who claimed, falsely, to be close to Trump and said he'd heard about a plan to blackmail Trump. They "reported" something everyone who uses Twitter knew—that the Russians were trying to sow division in the U.S. They found another source who said the Russians were feeding material to the Trump campaign. They researched Carter Page. They grabbed widely reported information about the WikiLeaks email dump being tied to the Russians and rewrote it. They heard a bunch of hooey about former Trump lawyer Michael Cohen traveling to Prague to pay off Russian hackers. And then Steele wrote it up and reported it as bombshell "raw intelligence."

All of it was plug-and-play. They plugged shocking allegations into the dossier, even though they knew it was the Mount Everest of horse manure. Then they fed it to Washington, which had been receiving reports from foreign intelligence services that also alleged connections between Trump and Russia. But those initial reports from intel services were problematic because you can't investigate American citizens without a warrant and because the FBI can't reliably discuss their provenance. But throw in explosive reports from a known and admired FBI informant like Christopher Steele and you now have the "evidence" to establish "probable cause" to start an investigation—an investigation that would leak and ultimately malign the Trump campaign.

Which was the goal of opposition research, and what I call Plan A.

Sure, George Papadopoulos, thanks or no thanks to Alexander Downer and U.K. intelligence, was in the FBI's sightlines in the summer of 2016. But so, *at exactly the same time*, was the Steele dossier. Bruce Ohr knew about it. Andrew McCabe knew about it. Peter Strzok knew about it. Glenn Simpson and Christopher Steele made sure they knew about it.

But the FBI management cabal running the Trump-team witch hunt said it didn't discuss ongoing investigations—except via selected leaks or when updating Congress. And when, as the election neared and there was no news of operation Crossfire Hurricane or the other shocking charges from Steele's reports, panic set in. It seems clear that Steele, and quite probably Simpson, began leaking. Michael Isikoff, Simpson's pal, wrote about Carter Page in September. Steele shared the dossier with David Corn at *Mother Jones* magazine.

In the height of irony and deviousness, Steele even managed to get the dossier to John McCain—alerting the candidate who knew intelligence agents had raised Russian-influencing operations to him during his own presidential campaign. They got the senior senator from the Republican Party to alert the FBI—a shrewd, compelling move because, of course, McCain was wary of Russians and he was in the same party as Trump. It was a politically deft "nonpolitical" move. You've heard of counterintelligence? This was counterpolitics: using a member of the right to help the members of the left. Brilliant, yes, but truly sleazy.

The story of the distribution of the dossier to McCain led to the wide leaking of the document to the mainstream press. Here is how it played out.

Barely a week after the 2016 election, Sir Andrew Wood, the former British ambassador to Russia, traveled to Canada to attend the Halifax International Security Forum. There he approached David Kramer, a longtime associate of John McCain, and made his pitch. Kramer recalls that Wood "was aware of information that he thought I should be aware of and that Senator McCain might be interested in." McCain was also at the conference. The three men met privately, and Wood briefed them on Steele's collusion concerns and mentioned the possibility that there was video "of a sexual nature" that might have "shown the president-elect in a compromising situation," according to Kramer's 2017 deposition for a lawsuit related to *BuzzFeed*'s publication of the dossier.[42]

At McCain's request, Kramer flew to London. He met Steele on November 28, 2016, and read the dossier. Returning to the States, he picked up copies of the dossier from Glenn Simpson, according to his testimony. He brought the dossier to McCain, who asked him to show it to a State Department official and a National Security Council official and determine if it was being vetted. Meanwhile, McCain himself shared the dossier with James Comey at the FBI.

As for sharing it elsewhere, during his deposition, Kramer admitted he gave copies of the dossier to reporters at *BuzzFeed*, McClatchy news service, the *Washington Post*, the *Wall Street Journal*, and National Public Radio.[43]

McCain even addressed his decision to share the document with Comey.

"I had an obligation to bring to the attention of appropriate officials unproven accusations I could not assess myself, and which, were any of them true, would create a vulnerability to the designs of a hostile foreign power," McCain writes in his 2018 memoir, *The Restless Wave*. "I discharged that obligation, and I would do it again. Anyone who doesn't like it can go to hell."[44]

McCain tried to make a case for raising his concerns. But unfortunately, he didn't realize that he was spun like a top. And he never realized that the entire purpose of the dossier, when it was shown to him, had evolved; now it was being used to force an investigation to take down the president-elect. And if he and his associates were truly interested in verifying the information, then why did his associate shamelessly leak the *unverified* allegations to the media? Why not simply give them to the FBI?

All these actions contributed to the narrative that Trump was compromised. They led to more aspersions and more suspicious news reports about the Trump team. They once again promoted the appearance of possible wrongdoing without actually proving that anything untoward happened. But it was nothing more than hype. Christopher Steele was just piling on, thanks in part to David Kramer's distributing the dossier to the media.

Of course, it was all old news at the FBI, where the investigation was already ongoing—and much of it was in the FISA warrant.

Christopher Steele had done his job. The chaos of Plan A had coalesced into Plan B. The investigators had the justification they needed to investigate collusion, cooperation, and conspiracy.

There was just one problem.

That justification, as we've just seen time and again, was total fiction. It wasn't even worth the paper it was printed on.

CHAPTER 5

The Run-Up

Now the aspersions had all been cast. The dossier had been manufactured. The FISA warrant application—which relied on the duplicate dossier reports that Steele fed to the FBI—had been issued.

What was the next step in bringing down the Trump campaign?

The answer was simple: the FBI management cabal targeting Trump now had to make good on its investigation.

To do that, presumably, all it had to do was follow the road map provided by Glenn Simpson, Christopher Steele, and their magical, FISA-court-fooling dossier. If anything in the dossier was verifiable regarding a Trump-Russia conspiracy, the FBI agents were just the guys to find the incontrovertible evidence needed to bring charges. The FBI is America's premier law enforcement agency. All agents had to do was find proof that the Russians had *kompromat* on Trump. Or that Carter Page was a spy. Or that Russia was trading information on Clinton to help the campaign. Find proof of one of those things and they would be on their way to the most explosive, frightening, critical investigation this side of Watergate, Monicagate, and all the other -gates put together.

I'm not joking here. If there was illegal influence, if a foreign power blackmailed a presidential candidate, if candidates were relying on outside support to cheat and steal in an election—all or any of that would be *huge* news. It would throw the nation into turmoil. It would destabilize the government, send tremors through Wall Street, and rattle the very bedrock of our country.

But, again, there's one important point, one key word in all these disturbing scenarios: "if."

The opposite of "if" is "if not." But that phrase doesn't appear in any of the FBI's thinking or the mainstream media's thinking.

But it should have appeared. Because the road map wasn't reliable; it was scarred with bogus directions and dead ends. Getting "there"—that is, arriving at hard, factual, verifiable, conviction-worthy evidence with no ifs, ands, or buts—wasn't going to be easy.

In fact, by the time the FISA warrant was issued, a lynchpin of the Russiagate myth was already imploding.

THINGS FALL APART

Once again, the story here relies on timing. So let's put the dossier and the FISA warrant to the side for a moment and revisit the tale of George Papadopoulos. I apologize if some of this feels repetitive, but it is important to establish what happened and when.

It is a fact that long before the Carter Page FISA warrant was issued, the FBI started investigating the collusion case against George Papadopoulos. We know this because the FBI still insists that the Papadopoulos case was the one that ignited Russiagate. Not the alleged communications from foreign intelligence in late 2015 and early 2016. Not Glenn Simpson's whispering in the ear of Bruce Ohr or Christopher Steele's meeting him for lunch. No, according to the FBI, it was George Papadopoulos, the young political rookie who had been living in London when he was named to the Trump advisory team.

Almost immediately upon joining the campaign—literally one day after he told colleagues he might be joining Team Trump—his boss in London told him to go to a conference in Rome. Papadopoulos didn't realize he was heading to one of Europe's most spy-friendly hangouts—Link Campus University—and when he showed up, he was introduced to Joseph Mifsud, a middle-aged spinmaster who allegedly told Papadopoulos he could help put the Trump campaign in touch with Russia. A few weeks later, Mifsud, who never actually delivered on any of his claims to Papadopoulos, showed up in London and allegedly revealed that the Russians have "dirt" on Hillary Clinton.

"Emails of Clinton," he said to Papadopoulos when they breakfasted at the Andaz hotel in London. "They have thousands of emails."[1]

According to the anti-Trump cabal's version of events, Mifsud is a Russian agent. According to Papadopoulos, Mifsud presented himself as having Russian connections but introduced him, via email, to only one person who had tangential Kremlin contacts. Papadopoulos considers Mifsud a fraud and a Western intelligence agent. According to Mifsud's millionaire friend and Swiss lawyer, Stephan Roh, mystery man Mifsud has ties to Western governments.[2] But for the moment, let's just accept the cabal's absurd designation that Mifsud's a Russian agent.

The formal investigation, operation Crossfire Hurricane, started on July 31, 2016. But by the middle of September, the FBI case against Papadopoulos was already disintegrating.

Papadopoulos's book, *Deep State Target*, reveals that on September 2, 2016, he got an "out of the blue" email invitation from Stefan Halper.[3] Remember him? He's the Western spy who appears to have launched allegations, in conjunction with his U.K. intelligence pal Richard Dearlove, about Lieutenant General Mike Flynn's being compromised for talking to a Russian woman at a Cambridge conference in 2014.

Halper offered Papadopoulos $3,000 plus expenses to fly to London to "discuss the Leviathan natural gas field."[4] Although Papadopoulos didn't know it at the time, Halper was working as a U.S. government informant. He also had made approaches to Carter Page and to Trump campaign bigwig Sam Clovis.

"I think [Halper] was using his meeting with me to give him bona fides to talk to George Papadopoulos," Clovis told the *Washington Examiner*. "He used Carter Page to get to me and he used me to get to George. George was the target. I think George was the target all along."[5]

When Papadopoulos unwittingly took the bait and showed up to meet with Halper, he was put through the wringer. First, Halper's attractive "research assistant," "Azra Turk," met Papadopoulos for drinks and possibly more. According to Papadopoulos, she was extremely touchy-feely at the bar, flirting while also asking him repeatedly about Trump and Russia and the campaign. Even after he told her directly, "I have nothing to do with Russia and don't know anyone else who has anything to do with Russia, either," she kept bringing up the campaign. Says Papadopoulos: "I'm thinking 'There is no way this is a Cambridge professor's research assistant. The only thing she seems to want to research is Trump, Russia, and me. I'm stunned by the come-hither tone of Azra Turk and her classic honey-pot act.'"[6]

It turns out Papadopoulos's suspicions were 100 percent correct. A May 2, 2019, article in the *New York Times* reports that sources confirmed that "Azra Turk" "was actually a government investigator posing as a research assistant…. The F.B.I. sent her to London as part of the counterintelligence inquiry opened that summer to better understand the Trump campaign's links to Russia."[7] The *Times* said its sources were "people familiar with the F.B.I. activities of Mr. Halper, Ms. Turk and" the DOJ inspector general's investigation into the FBI investigation.

Let's be clear: the *Times* does not clearly state that Azra Turk—which is likely a fake name—was working for the FBI, only that agents sent her there. Papadopoulos, for his part, has stated that he believes she was likely a CIA or Turkish intelligence recruit. Either way, the FBI needs to do a much better job choosing investigators. Papadopoulos quickly raised his suspicions during his two subsequent meetings with Halper. These encounters also veered into interrogations about the campaign and its work with Russia. As he recalls in his book, Halper posed the following types of questions:

> *It's great that Russia is helping you and the campaign, right, George?*
>
> *George, you and your campaign are involved in hacking and with Russia, right?*
>
> *It seems like you are a middleman for Trump and Russia, right?*
>
> *I know you know about the emails.*[8]

Papadopoulos finally grew furious with Halper's line of questioning. "What you are talking about is treason. And I have nothing to do with Russia, so stop bothering me about it."

The entire FBI operation to lure Papadopoulos into collusion charges fell apart right there, on the weekend of September 15–17, 2016. Azra Turk got nothing out of Papadopoulos and neither did Halper. Thousands of dollars must have been spent on this part of the operation—to pay Papadopoulos and his expenses as well as the operatives. For what? Papadopoulos was definitely a marked man—although it is still not clear who, exactly, first marked him. But no evidence has surfaced showing him to be a traitor. At no time was he conspiring or colluding. As he has consistently maintained, the campaign had told him they were interested in communicating with Russia and he was trying to make that happen. That was as far as he went. And when, allegedly, Mifsud told him about the emails, he never mentioned them in any subsequent emails or on any calls with the Trump campaign.

Papadopoulos has been criticized for not sharing that story or reporting Mifsud to the authorities. He says that helping the campaign arrange a meeting with Russians was the only thing he cared about. He had oversold his connections to the campaign and he wanted to follow through. "I don't ask about the emails," he writes. "I don't want to know, really. I don't really care. My mission is to make a meeting happen. End of story. Hacking, security breaches, potential blackmail—that is illegal and treasonous. I want no part of it."[9]

So the FBI knew in September 2016 that, barring a miracle, the Papadopoulos conspiracy angle was a flop. It had no evidence. No emails. No taped phone calls. No honey-pot-induced confessions. Nothing. There was no evidence that Papadopoulos did anything criminal as far as collusion is concerned. (In fact, reports later surfaced alleging that D.C. politicians had seen classified information indicating that there are "transcripts" of some of Papadopoulos's conversations that are "exculpatory.")

Can you imagine the panic in the FBI at this point? Operation Crossfire Hurricane had just shot itself in the foot. Now the only way to continue the probe was to double down on the allegations listed in the FISA warrant application.

And we all now know that the application was based on the reports Steele filed to the FBI, which sound remarkably similar to the reports in the dossier.

A FACTUAL INTERLUDE

Before we move on, I need to point something out.

Papadopoulos admits in his book that he did repeat Mifsud's claim to one and only one other person: the Greek foreign minister, Nikolaos Kotzias. During a visit to Athens on May 26, 2016, Kotzias told Papadopoulos that Putin would be in his office the next day. Papadopoulos decided to share what Mifsud had told him. "I've heard the Russians have Hillary Clinton's emails," he blurted out. According to the book, the foreign minister admonished Papadopoulos to never repeat what he'd just said, and Papadopoulos himself says he was immediately horrified by his own indiscretion.[10]

Was that conversation monitored? If so, who was listening? Did Kotzias report this to someone and was that conversation monitored?

This is something that has never been resolved. Because if Papadopoulos never told Downer or anyone else about Mifsud's email tale and he repeated the story of emails only once—while speaking Greek—then how did the FBI discover Mifsud's "Russia has Clinton dirt" claim, which was made months before news broke of the DNC email hack? Was Mifsud working with Western intel, as his online connections and as comments by his associates about his connections appear to indicate? Was Mifsud working with a political campaign, or a contractor being paid by a political campaign, as congressman Devin Nunes asked in a May 20, 2019, interview with Fox News's Shannon Bream?[11] Did he or his handlers feed information to intelligence operatives or the FBI?

Mifsud's connections and how the FBI learned of his email claims remain some of the most profound mysteries of Russiagate.

THE GRAND ILLUSION

The problem with the FBI's and the intelligence community's doubling down on the dossier (really quintupling down when you consider they swore to Steele's bogus information for an original FISA warrant, for three renewals, and in the December 2016 intelligence community assessment), as I spent the last chapter explaining, was the "raw intelligence" that comprised the document. It was as tainted and toxic and murky as, well, swamp water. The sourcing was unknown and therefore dubious, and the suspected sources we do know about, notably Trubnikov and Surkov, were specialists in Russian disinformation campaigns. Some of the "intelligence" seemed to follow relevant or tangential news reports, basically rehashing events and loosely tying them to Moscow.

In October 2016, then, armed with their FISA warrant, James Comey's lieutenants Peter Strzok, Bill Priestap, and other investigators set about trying to verify the claims made in the dossier—because those were the allegations used to obtain the warrant.

They investigated Carter Page. They worked with intelligence agencies to track Russian cyberoperations. They began interviewing members of the campaign. They did this all in secret because that's standard operating procedure at the bureau. Some of what they were investigating officially made it into press reports, but the dirty details of the investigation remained secret. While the dossier was leaked to David Corn, who reported on it prior to the election, the official FBI investigation continued in secret. On November 8, Trump pulled off one of the most shocking election victories in U.S. history. And on January 6, 2017, FBI director James Comey met with President-Elect Trump at Trump Tower.

This is where things get very nuanced and even more devious. At this point in time, the media knew about the dossier. In fact, a number of organizations had the dossier and were chomping at the bit to write about it. But they couldn't write about it because it was completely unverified and because, believe it or not, these organizations do adhere to certain standards out of fear of being dragged into a lawsuit. And writing a story about a document that is as reliable as graffiti scrawled on a bathroom wall understandably gave even the most Trump-hating organizations some pause. In other words, the press needed the dossier to become an official part of the story in order to report on it and damage Trump.

James Clapper, future CNN contributor, apparently knew this. Was this a motivating factor in his decision to advise Comey to brief Trump? It sure seems that way, especially if the House Intelligence Committee report I mentioned earlier was accurate when it stated: "Clapper subsequently acknowledged discussing the 'dossier with CNN journalist Jake Tapper,' and admitted that he might have spoken with other journalists about the same topic."[12]

But here's the catch: Comey didn't want to tell Trump about the entire dossier because the bureau was investigating the Trump campaign and he didn't want Trump to know that. By limiting his discussion to the salacious, ridiculous "pee tape" charges and the idea of blackmail, Comey avoided tipping off the future president to the fact that his entire campaign—including Trump, obviously—was under investigation, spurred by allegations that it colluded with Russia to win the election. So that's *all* Comey discussed with Trump: the pee stuff and the sex stuff. Not the other election-stealing, collusion allegations in the dossier or in any similar reports that Steele filed with the FBI.

I'm sure Comey and Clapper thought they were threading the needle here. Comey briefed Trump but didn't show all his cards; he made good on following the instructions from Clapper, who was the guru of government intelligence operations; and he maintained FBI policy by not clearly delineating the details of an ongoing investigation or even confirming its existence.

It was a remarkably shrewd and crafty move on his part. But there are other words for it, too: "misleading," "dishonest," "devious," "calculating," and "nasty" are some that come to mind.

At any rate, the exchange delivered just what Clapper needed for CNN. Although he denies being a source, evidence suggests he told Jake Tapper that the dossier was discussed, which was true in that *elements* of the dossier were discussed, and CNN and the rest of the world now had a hook on which to report on the "explosive" dossier.

There it was! The gates of hell opened wide and unleashed a torrent of charges that bordered on treason against the president-elect of the United States.

Trump was shocked and horrified. And so, frankly, was the rest of the world. These were stunning charges, the stuff of movies and spy thrillers. And they were gathered, we are told, by a "credible" FBI source who was in charge of Russian intelligence gathering for one of the world's most sophisticated intelligence organizations, England's MI6.

But no one was more outraged than Trump because he was put in a completely untenable position, which is often the plight of the wrongly accused.

He had no way to refute any of the charges except to say they didn't happen. The burden of proof is legally on investigators and the prosecution in our legal system. It isn't on the accused. But when sleazy allegations are made about you—things that never happened—how do you defend yourself? You are fighting shadows, ghosts, lies. No doubt, the natural inclination is to fight back, to rebut the falsehoods. But the charges in the dossier don't include the names of the accusers. They quite often don't even include specific details. So Trump really had no way of proving that the events in the dossier never happened.

There were no exchanges of damaging information that his campaign received, at least that he knew about. He's never been blackmailed by the Russians. That compromising videotape doesn't exist. All he could do is reject the claims. That's why he branded a great deal of what surfaced as "fake news." What else should you call it? I guess, if he wanted to take the high road, he could have called it irresponsible, unsubstantiated misinformation. But why play the euphemism game that the left and their media acolytes so adore? These were weaponized lies designed to hurt the Trump campaign and the future Trump administration. Whatever you call it, it all comes down to the same thing. Cooperation and collusion with Russia never happened under his direction or under the direction of anyone associated with Trump's campaign.

Listen, Trump is a maverick. He has said some things that the American public is not accustomed to hearing from our current crop of focus group-tested politicians. And any comments about Russia on the campaign trail were manna from heaven for his enemies looking to tar him with a fabricated collusion scandal.

But Trump never publicly walks back any of his past. That's not in his DNA, and being from Queens, New York, as Trump is, I understand that. But I think that if he could redo some of those things, he would. Like it or not, they gave his corrupt adversaries ammunition; they helped create the optics—the appearance—that Trump was eager to work with Russia.

Still, the investigation, based on hearsay, was frustrating and infuriating to Trump. And that wasn't his only headache. Maverick military man Michael Flynn had been working as an advisor to Trump since February 2016. By November, the retired three-star general had impressed Trump enough to be tapped as the president-elect's national security advisor. But Flynn quickly became a target as reports surfaced of his lobbying efforts on behalf of Turkey. And those reports were soon overtaken by a series of leaks and reports about Flynn's communications with then Russian ambassador Sergey Kislyak—the very same man named in the Steele dossier who would, as we are about to see, also haunt Jeff Sessions.

Kislyak haunted Flynn. Big-time. But so did the press, who relayed leaks about Flynn's conversations with Kislyak *and* Flynn's conversations with the FBI.

According to a partially redacted FBI memo, Flynn "did not give any indicators of deception" when bureau agents interviewed him on January 24, 2017, about the specifics of his calls with Kislyak. Reliable information that I am privy to indicates that Flynn was not lying about the details of his call with Kislyak in his conversations with FBI agents Peter Strzok and Joe Pientka, and that Flynn was simply not able to recall certain details due to the time and place of the conversation and the circumstances surrounding the call. But things snowballed from there, with the press smelling blood and continuing to pile on.

Once again, optics—the appearance of *possible* impropriety and subsequently weaponized PR—cursed Team Trump. Sally Yates, then-acting attorney general and noted anti-Trump cheerleader, learned about Flynn's FBI interview. News then leaked that she warned White House counsel Don McGahn in January 2017 that Flynn's denial of discussing sanctions with Kislyak may have been misleading, and that Flynn's comments made him "vulnerable to Russian blackmail."[13]

It's hard not to wonder if Flynn still had a target on his back from his time with the Obama administration. Obama had in 2013 fired Flynn from his job as head of the DIA. And when Trump met with the departing president in the Oval Office on November 10, 2016, Obama actually warned Trump about working with Flynn and said he "wasn't exactly a fan" of Flynn, according to former White House Press Secretary Sean Spicer.[14]

Blackmail. Russia. Trump advisor. Obama foe. Does any of this sound familiar? It sure does. This is the same kind of garbage that filled the dossier. There is no evidence that Flynn was ever blackmailed, and using the Logan Act—the 1799 law forbidding unauthorized communication with foreign governments, violations of which had never been successfully prosecuted—as a precedent to pressure the Trump team to get rid of Flynn, as Yates did, was absurd, even by D.C. swamp standards. Even more outrageous is the idea that the Russians thought they could leverage this and turn a former three-star general into a treasonous spy. But that was the narrative that the mainstream media bought—hook, line, and sinker. Throw in the story about Flynn's getting paid a reported $40,000 to speak at a 2015 gala for RT, the Russian TV network, where he sat at a table with Russian president Vladimir Putin, and Flynn had no chance at political survival. The swamp was hungry for a scalp. The optics increased the volume for the Collusion Chorus and Flynn was finished. He was forced to resign on February 13, 2017.

The Flynn debacle played out directly under the shadow of the now-debunked dossier, which was posted online by *BuzzFeed* on January 10, 2017, putting the entire misinformation-filled document in the public view. It was excerpted everywhere. The world was treated to thousands of articles, posts, and tweets about sleazy, disgusting stories and about the dossier author, Christopher Steele. To the anti-Trump brigade, he was the second coming of James Bond—an upstanding

Russia specialist with impeccable sources and an unassailable reputation. But he was really James Bonehead and nothing more than a sad, sorry, has-been gossiper profiting off of lies and misinformation. He was the prototypical "useful idiot."

The *BuzzFeed* posting gave credibility to what was a totally incredible dossier in the eyes of those desperate to find chum in the water when no such water existed in the first place. And instead of disavowing the filthy dossier and Steele's information, the premier law enforcement agency on the planet was investigating Steele's information. In fact, to get a FISA warrant, agents swore to its legitimacy and placed the word, in all caps, "verified" on the FISA warrant application used to spy on the Trump team. It was all a gross abuse of misinformation.

Privately, Trump fumed to any and all around him about what he called, over and over and over, a "witch hunt." He told his communications lead Hope Hicks that the idea that the Russians helped him win the election was crippling.[15] According to Sean Spicer, Trump's first White House spokesman, the president believed that the Russia story had been developed to undermine the legitimacy of his election.[16] It delegitimized his triumph. It took the shine off one of the greatest political upset stories in American history. You can see why this was extremely important to him. All presidents want to know they have the support of the nation behind them. It's both human nature and political nature. Polls help policy get through Congress. Public opinion, while not the only policy driver, is a useful mirror for politicians. The allegations polarized America. They still do. And that has made governing much harder.

One of the ironic things about the investigation into Russiagate is that Trump actually told James Comey that making sure his campaign and administration were on the up-and-up would be a good thing. (Does that sound like "obstruction of justice" to you? Yeah, me neither.)

Comey's June 8, 2016, testimony to the Senate Intelligence Committee reveals that during his call with the president on March 30, 2017,

Trump said he was fine with investigators reviewing the conduct of the people around him.

"Trump went on to say that if there were some 'satellite' associates who did something wrong, it would be good to find that out, but that he hadn't done anything wrong and hoped we would find some way of getting it out that we weren't investigating him," Comey said in his opening statement.[17]

Trump's interaction with Comey grew more problematic, as the world knows. But Comey was hardly the only one who infuriated the president.

Attorney General Jeff Sessions, a longtime Trump ally, also angered the president. During his Senate confirmation hearing in January 2017, Sessions failed to reveal that he'd briefly met Russian ambassador Kislyak and insisted to the Senate that he "did not have communications with the Russians." Mueller later vindicated Sessions by acknowledging these were not meetings but mere brief encounters.

Once it was discovered that Sessions had failed to recall brief encounters, which are not even remotely unusual for a politician of Session's stature, with Kislyak—one during an event at the Republican National Convention in Cleveland and another on September 8[18]—the attorney general was engulfed in a cloud of suspicion of disingenuous collusion. Once again, the optics, as if bent in a funhouse mirror, were twisted to make it look like Sessions was hiding something. And so, for optics, he recused himself from overseeing the Russiagate investigation at the Department of Justice. He then appointed Rod Rosenstein to handle things.

Big mistake.

Sessions's decision to recuse himself was yet another capitulation to the optics created by the toxic climate of distrust sown by Steele, the dossier, and the echo chamber of the mainstream media. Seriously, if Moscow had wanted to divide the country, create turmoil, and destabilize the presidency, they probably couldn't have done it any better than Glenn Simpson, Christopher Steele, and the reporters who bit on their bogus "intel." The chief lawman was forced to abdicate control of the most important investigation in American history because he stopped for a handshake with the chief Russian diplomat in America.

Trump couldn't believe that Sessions, an early Trump adopter on Capitol Hill, had ceded control. He was apoplectic over it. A guy he presumed would be his right-hand man would have no insight into the illegitimate investigation and also would have no influence.

More leaks sprung. Or maybe we should call them "hits." On February 14, the day after Flynn's resignation, the *New York Times* reported that "four current and former officials" said, "Phone records and intercepted calls show that members of Donald J. Trump's 2016 presidential campaign and other Trump associates had repeated contacts with senior Russian intelligence officials in the year before the election."[19]

Obviously, those sources were as accurate as Christopher Steele's fabricators, right? Who were these sources? Who were the Trump associates? Just as with the Steele dossier, the charges here were *unverified.* We now know that Carter Page was targeted by Russian spooks, who later deemed him unworthy of being an asset. But that's it. Manafort and Flynn did not meet with "senior Russian intelligence officials." Nobody has shown that Mifsud was working for Russia, and Mifsud was never charged with a crime. Mifsud was even allowed back into the United States in February 2017 to attend a conference at which the State Department was a sponsor. As noted previously, Papadopoulos is convinced that Mifsud was working with Western intelligence, and the evidence of Mifsud's connections to Western intelligence can be at your fingertips using a simple image search on the internet.

What should have been a honeymoon period for a new presidency was a partial nightmare. During its early months, the administration was faced with courts rolling back Trump's immigration policies. Stories abounded in the anti-Trump press regarding dysfunction in the White House—stories about a shortage of appointees, unfilled positions, and icy relations with traditional American allies. But the thing that truly rankled the president was the idea that his election was not legitimate. That some nonexistent secret agreement with Russia had put him in office.

The one man who could have ended all the specious speculation, all the unproven, unsubstantiated, and untrue allegations, was James Comey, the FBI director appointed by Obama who had repeatedly told Trump he was not under investigation. But the character-free Comey took the easy path instead of the right one. And he let the media rumors fester like an open sore.

And then, on March 20, 2017, testifying before the House Intelligence Committee, Comey reversed course, making it clear that the Trump campaign was, in fact, under an investigative microscope:

> I've been authorized by the Department of Justice to confirm that the FBI, as part of our counterintelligence mission, is investigating the Russian government's efforts to interfere in the 2016 presidential election. That includes investigating the nature of any links between individuals associated with the Trump campaign and the Russian government, and whether there was any coordination between the campaign and Russia's efforts. As with any counterintelligence investigation, this will also include an assessment of whether any crimes were committed. Because it is an open, ongoing investigation, and is classified, I cannot say more about what we are doing and whose conduct we are examining.[20]

On one level, Trump may have found this reassuring. But on another, it must have seemed ominous. He knew that the FBI was investigating his campaign. He had no control over what any of those interviewed might say. He also knew from experience—just look at the dossier—that anyone could say anything about him, and that the FBI might take utter lies as the truth. It was nuts. He was a victim of a completely maddening set of circumstances. And the fallout from all the allegations and aspersions was crippling. His administration and the entire Republican Party were being wounded on a daily basis in the media mosh pit over Russiagate fantasies.

Did Trump speak out and complain about all of this? Of course. He was anything but shy about his frustration. He even took to Twitter—the most public of forums—to express his disgust. It is no surprise that he wanted to stop the bleeding from a confirmed witch hunt that was based on opposition research paid for by Hillary Clinton and the DNC.

He wanted the false narrative to end but there was no end in sight.

On May 9, 2017, asserting his right as the president of the United States to appoint and to fire the director of the Federal Bureau of Investigation, Trump axed Comey.

If the president thought this move would allow his administration to flourish and allow him to regain his reputation, he was sorely mistaken. By firing Comey, Trump unwittingly ignited another firestorm, opening another front in a partisan war.

This was no longer just about Russiagate. This was about the FBI's and the DOJ's reputations. The Russiagate investigation had been going on for ten months. So far, not a shred of evidence confirming a conspiracy had been uncovered. Papadopoulos had been interviewed and had delivered nothing because there was nothing to deliver. Flynn was in trouble on a number of potential charges, but none of them involved coordination with Russia and the campaign. And Manafort was tied to a laundry list of criminal and financial crimes—but none involved the campaign. Investigators had nothing but rumors, appearances, and coincidences. The scandal, truth be told, was that there was no scandal. And that was a *big* problem for our premier law enforcement divisions.

This was the reality, then, that launched Plan C.

The dossier and Steele's reports to the FBI were now going to be more important than ever.

CHAPTER 6

Plan C: Operation Save the FBI From Itself

Trump's decision to banish James Comey was completely justified. Under Comey, the bureau completely mishandled the Hillary Clinton email investigation from its start to its inglorious finish. And as we've seen, the FBI's handling of Russiagate was completely inept and tainted by pro-Clinton agents idiotically texting their own biases to one another over unclassified and discoverable electronic devices. Plus, Comey repeatedly lied to the president he was serving, telling Trump he wasn't under investigation.

Trump may have drawn momentary comfort from Comey's assurances at one point. But Comey's claims were a laughable deflection of the truth. When a candidate's campaign is under investigation, you can bet the candidate is under investigation, too. Everyone in the campaign is a stone's throw away from the man in charge. There is no way anyone could honestly say with a straight face that Trump was not being investigated.

Except, of course, the inept James Comey.

In addition, we know now that Comey wrote memos every time he met with Trump, documenting, in his mind, possible attempts at obstruction. Why was he writing memos about these encounters? Was Comey some kind of avid diarist? Did he compulsively document all of his encounters with Obama? No, he did not. Comey even told the Senate Intelligence Committee on March 20, 2017, that he didn't "memorialize" anything Obama said. But with Trump, things were different:

> *I felt compelled to document my first conversation with the President-Elect in a memo. To ensure accuracy, I began to type it on a laptop in an FBI vehicle outside Trump Tower the moment I walked out of the meeting. Creating written records immediately after one-on-one conversations with Mr. Trump was my practice from that point forward. This had not been my practice in the past. I spoke alone with President Obama twice in person (and never on the phone)—once in 2015 to discuss law enforcement policy issues and a second time, briefly, for him to say goodbye in late 2016. In neither of those circumstances did I memorialize the discussions.*[1]

So Comey was writing up his Trump encounters—which, again, I'm sure that Trump, who was new to the office and the protocols that go with it, wishes he had dealt with differently—*for possible future legal action.*

In other words, Comey may not have been formally investigating Trump, but he was clearly stockpiling evidence to advance his rogue investigation and his personal vendetta.

You know what I think about Comey and his memos? He abused his power and used his detailed knowledge of the destructive games played by D.C. swamp rats to set up Trump. On a normal day, the president likes to shake things up, create disturbances to keep everyone humming and to be his usual unedited man of action. That's how he rolls. We've all seen it. And Comey, who was very guarded around Trump and very dishonest—at least when it came to revealing the dossier contents and the extent of the investigation—knew this. He had seen that the president was actually bothered, annoyed, and crippled by Russiagate on that very first meeting. Comey was, in essence, setting a trap for Trump.

One day after firing Comey, as Democrats began constructing a false obstruction narrative that Comey had been fired to stem the Russiagate investigation, Trump spoke up about Comey. While hosting Russia's foreign minister, Sergey V. Lavrov, and Ambassador Kislyak in a May 10, 2017, meeting in the Oval Office, the president told his visitors that firing FBI director Comey had relieved "great pressure."

"I just fired the head of the FBI. He was crazy, a real nutjob," Trump said, according to a summary document of the meeting.[2] "I faced great pressure because of Russia. That's taken off."

Trump added, "I'm not under investigation."

Instantly, his enemies pounced again. This was treated by Never Trumpers and the left-wing media as explosive news.[3] But was it really any surprise that Trump was relieved by the removal of Comey? Trump is the guy who fired him! Of course, he wanted Comey gone. News flash: *that's why he fired him*!

Being a straight shooter is a great thing in politics. We need more people who will tell the unvarnished truth. But when your enemies are hell-bent on destroying you and eager to set you up, telling it like it is can be downright dangerous because your words will be twisted to be used against you. Trump's statements about firing Comey were a gift to anyone who wanted to float an obstruction fairy tale. And that's just how they were used.

MUELLER GOES INTO THE BREACH

Comey didn't exactly go quietly. He started leaking notes through a friend—something he actually admitted in a hearing. On May 11, the *New York Times* ran a story saying Trump had demanded loyalty from Comey.[4] Big deal! Isn't that a given? Shouldn't a president want a loyal staff? What did that prove? Then, on May 16, the *New York Times* published an article about memos by Comey. This is how it began:

> President Trump asked the F.B.I. director, James B. Comey, to shut down the federal investigation into Mr. Trump's former national security adviser, Michael T. Flynn, in an Oval Office meeting in February, according to a memo Mr. Comey wrote shortly after the meeting.[5]

Of course, this is completely debatable, slanted reporting. What the president actually said to Comey, according to the article and according to the memo, was: "I hope you can see your way clear to letting this go, to letting Flynn go.... He is a good guy. I hope you can let this go."

Times reporter Michael S. Schmidt was clearly sensationalizing the quote. Trump didn't ask Comey to do anything. Trump was stating a wish. It was not a directive. It was not an order. It was not a query or a request. How Schmidt and the *New York Times* arrived at Trump's asking Comey to shut down an investigation that was never shut down is quite a leap.

All Comey's memos of meetings with Trump allege that the president said a number of things regarding FBI investigations—but they were things that could be open to interpretation. The media loves writing about this Comey stuff, and they use it to paint the president in a completely negative light. As acting FBI director, Andrew McCabe—whose wife, Jill, lost the 2015 Democratic Virginia state senator bid despite the help of Virginia governor and former Hillary Clinton consigliere Terry McAuliffe—convened a meeting with his Russiagate team. He also claims in his book, *The Threat*, that he met with Rod Rosenstein to review investigation options. At some point, the idea of opening a new avenue of the Russiagate investigation was broached: *probing the president of the United States on obstruction-of-justice charges.*

McCabe then met with the "Gang of Eight," a bipartisan group of senators and congressmen who work on intelligence issues, to broach the obstruction angle. "In that process, no one [objected to the investigation]," he says. "The leadership on the Hill did not disagree."[6]

McCabe obviously took this as a green light. The president was officially, but not publicly, a target of the FBI.

Meanwhile, with the Comey firing and the Comey memo leaks, along with the relentless dossier coverage, calls for a special investigation began to intensify. The anti-Trump brigade was now approaching peak hysteria.

Remember, at this point Jeff Sessions had already recused himself, much to Trump's dismay, because he was worried that his failure to recall a series of mundane interactions with Russian ambassador Kislyak made him appear compromised. So Rod Rosenstein, the recently minted deputy attorney general, was made the acting attorney general as far as the Russiagate investigation was concerned. Sessions and Trump asked Rosenstein, who was appointed to his new gig in April, to draft a memo that listed the ways Comey had played fast and loose with Justice Department protocols leading up to the 2016 election. They then used that memo as exhibit #1 for firing Comey. Was Rosenstein happy about this?

He says he has no regrets. But stories have surfaced that he was furious about being used as the author of Comey's demise. It made him look bad in the D.C. swamp, especially at FBI headquarters, where Comey still retained some support.[7] In fact, Rosenstein now had to work with McCabe, who counted Comey as a pal. Meanwhile, the outcry regarding Comey's leaks about what the president supposedly said was getting louder and louder. Democrats began calling for an independent investigator—and they threatened to deny a vote to confirm a successor to Comey until their demands were met.

Rosenstein could have refused. He could have called Comey's firing what it was—the president's exercising his right to appoint and fire the FBI director. He could have called Russiagate what it was: a weaponized witch hunt. He could have called the Democrats' bluff. Some legal experts say that when Trump had him draft the "fire Comey" memo, Trump inadvertently made Rosenstein part of the removal procedure, which meant he was obligated to appoint someone else to manage the inquiry.[8]

Almost, but not quite.

The guy had been on the job a month. He was thrown into the hot seat. Too bad everybody got burned.

Here's my take on Rosenstein. The guy, as I've said, is a company man with more than two decades as a government lawyer, but he was a political novice who was basically destroyed by his time in the spotlight. When he showed up as assistant attorney general and was asked to write the memo to fire Comey, he probably never expected his Comey-critique would ignite a major firestorm. This is understandable. Back in November 2016, after Comey reignited the Clinton email investigation just days before the election, the FBI director was public enemy #1 among Democrats. He was absolutely *loathed* as the guy who handed Trump the election by dragging Clinton down when he reopened the investigation into her email server misuse. So Rosenstein might have thought he was going to be a hero to the D.C. swamp denizens for calling Comey out.

But the narrative on Comey had somehow shifted, as the sleazy, dishonest FBI director managed to spin himself as the last bastion between Trump and the rule of law. And when Comey was fired, Rosenstein wasn't a hero; he was suddenly a villain. A Judas. So he burned Comey, but somehow he felt burned by Sessions and Trump, who used his input to fire Comey. How much allegiance and gratitude did this career lawman now feel toward his bosses? Probably not very much.

It's likely that Rosenstein, conflicted about his bosses, looked for guidance. He consulted the law on appointing a special counsel:

> § 600.1 *Grounds for appointing a Special Counsel.*
> *The Attorney General, or in cases in which the Attorney General is recused, the Acting Attorney General, will appoint a Special Counsel*

when he or she determines that criminal investigation of a person or matter is warranted and -

(a) That investigation or prosecution of that person or matter by a United States Attorney's Office or litigating Division of the Department of Justice would present a conflict of interest for the Department or other extraordinary circumstances; and

(b) That under the circumstances, it would be in the public interest to appoint an outside Special Counsel to assume responsibility for the matter.

Now here's the part of the law that offered Rosenstein other options.

§ 600.2 Alternatives available to the Attorney General.

When matters are brought to the attention of the Attorney General that might warrant consideration of appointment of a Special Counsel, the Attorney General may:

(a) Appoint a Special Counsel;

(b) Direct that an initial investigation, consisting of such factual inquiry or legal research as the Attorney General deems appropriate, be conducted in order to better inform the decision; or

(c) Conclude that under the circumstances of the matter, the public interest would not be served by removing the investigation from the normal processes of the Department, and that the appropriate component of the Department should handle the matter. If the Attorney General reaches this conclusion, he or she may direct that appropriate steps be taken to mitigate any conflicts of interest, such as recusal of particular officials.[9]

So you can see, Rod Rosenstein didn't have to appoint anybody. He could have said, "Hey, the buck stops here." He didn't. Why not? Yes, the pressure was intense. The Comey memo leaks had done just what they were intended to do: increase the aura of suspicion around the president and make the nation doubt his legitimacy.

And although Rosenstein could have counteracted Comey's assault by telling the FBI to finish up its investigation and issue its findings, he didn't do that, either. He capitulated to Comey and the Democrats, and yes, even to some Republicans who wanted the Russiagate investigations expanded. Why did he make that choice?

Obviously, as with so much of Russiagate, he was influenced by appearances, by the portrait Comey had created through his testimony and his leaks, which came on top of Sally Yates's testimony, the leaks on Flynn, and so many other mysterious leaks by Obama loyalists. And, yes, I think he was ticked off at being made the fall guy for ousting Comey. But I think there was something else driving him: loyalty to the FBI and to his old friend Robert Mueller.

The Department of Justice works often in lockstep with the FBI. The bureau does a great deal of the legwork and "gets their man," as the old expression goes. The DOJ then gets the conviction. As the FBI's own website describes the relationship: "Within the U.S. Department of Justice, the FBI is responsible to the attorney general, and it reports its findings to U.S. Attorneys across the country."[10] So there is a kind of symbiotic relationship between the DOJ and the FBI. They need each other. They are family.

Now the famous FBI had been compromised by atrocious management decisions. Its reputation—which, to this day, is periodically damaged by continuing revelations that former director J. Edgar Hoover spied and conducted hostile operations against U.S. citizens—was hanging in the balance. Its director, Comey, had just been humiliated. And that director, in turn, leaked obstruction-tinged stories to humiliate the president, who was under investigation.

Rod Rosenstein must have received briefings on the Russiagate investigation, which had been officially going on for ten months at this point. He met with McCabe. Presumably, he must have talked to investigators. There's little chance he wasn't told about the FISA warrant applications on Carter Page that Comey had signed multiple times. Rosenstein has always been suspiciously cryptic about how much detail he got about Steele, the dossier, Steele's relationship with Glenn

Simpson, and Steele and Simpson's relationship to Hillary Clinton. He must have been briefed, you'd hope, that interviews with George Papadopoulos had yielded no evidence of collusion, and that they had even produced exculpatory evidence. You'd expect him to meet with Peter Strzok, the head of the FBI counterintelligence investigation at the time. Strzok, as we know now from his texts to Lisa Page (his gal pal and an FBI lawyer), disliked Trump but also thought there was "no there there" when it came to Russiagate. Did he tell that to Rod Rosenstein? Was the brand-new deputy attorney general fed the full story or just half the story? If his top-line briefings just skimmed the surface, if they recounted the crap in the dossier and avoided addressing the potentially compromised relationships that created the dossier— among Simpson, Steele, Clinton, Trubnikov, Surkov, the DNC, and other unnamed sources—then, of course, he would approve a special counsel. He'd be swayed like all the other liberal, mainstream players who saw a harmless spark and shouted "fire," and who were blinded by their hatred of Trump, his business as unusual agenda, and his campaign remarks.

Rosenstein, as noted, is a company man. He wanted the company to be redeemed. The DOJ needs the FBI. With his boss Jeff Sessions recused from all things Russian, Rosenstein had to make a decision. He wound up buying what the FBI was selling and what the obsessed liberals were yelling.

And he had the perfect man for the job that needed to be done: one of his role models, Robert Mueller.

I'm not kidding. Back in 2005, when he was named Maryland's newest U.S. attorney, Rosenstein gave an interview to the *Maryland Daily Record*. He was asked who his role models were. He named only one man. Here's his full answer:

> *I've been fortunate to have many over the course of my career. One is [Robert Mueller], the head of the FBI. My first job in law enforcement*

*was as an intern in the U.S. Attorney's Office in Boston, when Mueller
was the interim U.S. attorney up there. I then came to Washington,
and I wound up working in the criminal division of the Justice
Department [then headed by Mueller]. He was a career prosecutor,
someone who was respected for his legal judgment and who was
never thought of as being a partisan prosecutor. It's really critical that
people, when they deal with the U.S. attorney's office, have a right to
expect that they are going to be treated without regard to politics. I
think it's important that we do everything we can to reassure people
that that's going to be the case.*[11]

I'm sure some readers find some of Rosenstein's words ironic,
considering that he, and his choice for special counsel, dragged out
a politically tainted investigation for nearly two years. I know I do.
But more than that, I also believe Rosenstein. I think he was speaking
honestly. As I said, he's a company guy. A lifetime government lawyer.
Rosenstein believes in the institution of government. The Department of Justice was his church. He had devoted his life to it. And
Robert Mueller, Rosenstein's role model, had served two churches: the
DOJ and the FBI.

Both departments were understandably under fire from the president of the United States. I believe both men felt that the institutions
they believed in were under attack. The president was accusing the
FBI of being partisan—the opposite of being impartial, which was
the very thing Rosenstein believed was of paramount importance,
the thing he believed Robert Mueller personified. Meanwhile, Rosenstein, thanks to the memo he wrote at Trump's request, was perceived
by many in the bureau as being anti-Comey. Hiring Mueller, the
former FBI head, to run the investigation as special counsel must have
seemed like the best of both worlds. Mueller was a G-man who was
a former prosecutor and a Republican. He was upstanding enough
to withstand any suggestion of impropriety or bias. You can see how
Rosenstein though Mueller was just the guy to remove any clouds of
suspicion engulfing D.C.

CLOUD CONFUSION

There was one problem with those clouds. There was one hanging over the FBI and there was one hanging over the White House. Which was more ominous and threatening to Mueller and Rosenstein?

Rosenstein brought Mueller over to the Oval Office for a meeting with the president and Sessions. It has been reported that this was an interview of sorts, that Trump was considering Mueller as a replacement for Comey. But as I alluded to earlier, I think that wasn't the case. I think Rosenstein, who was shocked and appalled by Trump's unapologetic behavior, and who was annoyed about drafting the memo that the president used to justify firing Comey, wanted Mueller to meet with Trump. He knew the buttoned-up, conservative former FBI director would be suspicious.

The next day, Mueller took the job Rosenstein offered. He had no interest in working for the president. He was interested in working for nobody but Rosenstein and covering for his old stomping grounds. He would investigate the man who had just interviewed him as well as the campaign and the rumors against it. The cloud over the White House wasn't going anywhere until the cloud over his old house—the J. Edgar Hoover Building, home to the FBI—dissipated.

That, I believe, was the premise of the Mueller investigation, both for Rosenstein and his hero appointee. The initial appointment document lays this out, directly tying Mueller's future work to the investigation started under Comey.

Appointment of Special Counsel
to Investigate Russian Interference With the
2016 Presidential Election and Related Matters

By virtue of the authority vested in me as Acting Attorney General, including 28 U.S.C. §§ 509, 510, and 515, in order to discharge my responsibility to provide supervision and of the Department of Justice, and to ensure a full and thorough investigation of the Russian government's efforts to interfere in the 2016 presidential election, I hereby order as follows:

(a) Robert S. Mueller III is appointed to serve as Special Counsel for the United States Department of Justice.

(b) The Special Counsel is authorized to conduct the investigation confirmed by then-FBI Director James B. Comey in testimony before the House Permanent Select Committee on Intelligence on March 20, 2017, including:

(i) any links and/or coordination between the Russian government and individuals associated with the campaign of President Donald Trump; and

(ii) any matters that arose or may arise directly from the investigation; and

(iii) any other matters within the scope of 28 C.F.R. § 600.4(a).

(c) If the Special Counsel believes it is necessary and appropriate, the Special Counsel is authorized to prosecute federal crimes arising from the investigation of these matters.[12]

As you can see, the appointment of Mueller doesn't make even the smallest nod to Trump's charges of harassment or targeting. From this perspective, there is no cloud over the FBI. It is blue sky all the way. And why not? In a face-off between the Trump campaign and the misinformation campaign, the latter, in conjunction with media allies, had been slaughtering the former. And with Mueller in place, that trend was primed to continue.

But it wasn't going to be easy.

DREAM TEAM ASSEMBLY

Right away, law and order poster boy Robert Mueller, hailed by so many as the savior of the Republic, began assembling his prosecution dream team. It was like a fantasy-league draft for legal nerds. Actually, make that Clinton-loving legal nerds, because Mueller wound up drafting a team loaded with liberal ringers! I gave you a partial rundown in

Chapter 2: at least two avowed Clinton campaign donors, a Sally Yates fanboy, haters of big business, and on and on. Plus, Mueller appointed Peter Strzok as his lead investigator. At this point, Strzok was regarded as the most up-to-date investigator on Russiagate. He headed the counterintelligence investigation for the FBI. As such, he presumably knew the backstory on every footnote, every dotted "i" and every crossed "t" in the FISA warrant application.

He must have seemed like the key player to Mueller. The puzzle master. The spy breaker. Strzok knew all there was to know about the timeline of the probe. He knew about the intel. He knew about Papadopoulos, Page, and Manafort. He even interviewed Mike Flynn in the Oval Office. He knew everyone—including CIA head John Brennan, whom he would reportedly brief.

It's not clear whether Mueller knew that Strzok was involved in a romantic relationship with FBI lawyer Lisa Page, but he drafted her on to the dream team—I want to write "scheme team"—too. After all, she knew the legal guidelines that the FBI had been operating within, or possibly skirting, to conduct its all-out inquiry.

It took less than two months for Peter Strzok and Lisa Page to go from investigation superstars to black sheep.

The event was the wake-up call Rosenstein should have gotten before he turned to Mueller, and that Mueller should have gotten before he accepted the special counsel gig. But it came too late. The two men controlling the future of Russiagate were now in too deep.

Way over their heads, in fact.

STRZOK'S FATAL ERRORS

On January 11, 2017, Justice Department Inspector General Michael Horowitz, who took the job in 2012 under the Obama administration, began an investigation into misconduct allegations involving FBI director Comey and how he handled the probe of Hillary Clinton's email practices. The investigation was extremely broad and included sweeps of inter-FBI communications, including email and texts on agency-issued phones.

Among the players Horowitz probed were Peter Strzok, who had been assigned from August 2015 until July 2016 to the FBI's investigation of Hillary Clinton's use of a private email server, and Lisa Page, who was FBI deputy director Andrew McCabe's special counsel during the same period. Since Comey reopened the Clinton email investigation around October 28, 2016, and closed it on November 6, 2016, the relevant dates overlapped a bit with Strzok's work investigating allegations of Russian interference in the 2016 election, which Lisa Page was involved in as well.

Naturally, Horowitz wanted to see the communications between these major figures in the investigation. However, according to DOJ Assistant Attorney General Stephen E. Boyd in a letter, the FBI's technical system for retaining text messages sent and received on FBI mobile devices questionably failed to preserve text messages for Strzok and Page from December 14, 2016, to approximately May 17, 2017. The letter indicates that the collection tool failure was due to "'misconfiguration issues related to rollouts, provisioning, and software upgrades that conflicted with the FBI's collection capabilities."[13]

By July 2017, Horowitz's team had uncovered disturbing texts between Strzok and Page. Eventually, the inspector general's team would use digital forensic methods to recover almost 20,000 texts—9,311 messages from Strzok's iPhone and 10,760 from Page's—from the collection tool "failure" period.[14] The content of the messages varies, from the mundane and managerial to the mercenary and maniacal.

We've already covered some of their exchanges. And Strzok made national headlines by referring to Trump as an "idiot" and worse. He told Page, "[W]e'll stop" Trump from being elected, and he also texted: "I'm afraid we can't take that risk [of Trump's winning]. It's like an insurance policy in the unlikely event you die before you're 40."

There are many more shocking exchanges uncovered by the inspector general. The couple also texted with lead DOJ inquisitor Kevin Clinesmith, who was handling the Papadopoulos inquiry for Team Mueller. When Clinesmith joined in on their Trump trashing, texting, "Viva le resistance! [sic]" he found himself off the investigation.[15]

This is toxic, embarrassing stuff. It makes the FBI investigation into Russiagate look like a targeted political witch hunt, not a professional FBI investigation. And it also, obviously, makes Mueller's special counsel investigation look awful. Strzok comes off as an unabashed partisan. He represents the exact opposite of what Rod Rosenstein aspired to back in 2005 when he talked about Mueller and about how it was so important that citizens who deal with the U.S. Attorney's Office "have a right to expect that they are going to be treated without regard to politics," and about how he strives to "do everything we can to reassure people that that's going to be the case." So Strzok was transferred back to the FBI and placed in the human resources department. He toiled in oblivion until he was fired on August 10, 2018. Page was also bounced from the Mueller team. She resigned from the FBI on May 4, 2018.

At the time Page and Strzok were banished, the precise reasons were kept under wraps. The Mueller team didn't release a statement saying they had compromised the integrity of the Trump-Russia investigation, obviously. Instead, Strzok and Page just quietly disappeared. But Mueller and Rosenstein knew it was just a matter of time before word leaked out about their scurrilous, compromising texts. After months of the FBI foisting bad optics on Trump, the whistle was finally about to be blown on the FBI. The investigation that brought down Comey was now going to be examined anew and the results would likely be damning—if not totally indefensible. The lead counterintelligence officer for the FBI:

    a. **was completely indiscreet about his opinions and the workings of the bureau;**

b. was a foul-mouthed, unapologetic Trump hater; and, most damningly,

c. didn't actually believe there was any evidence of Trump-Russia collusion—"There's no there," remember?—which is what the entire special counsel investigation was based on.

Now Mueller and Rosenstein had to make a decision. Had the unmasking of Strzok's texts and his unconscionable behavior compromised the integrity of the Trump-Russia probe? Was the special counsel a dead man walking because of it?

Evidently, they evaluated the situation and somehow decided they still had a viable witch hunt and didn't need to wave a white flag. The special counsel was two months into the investigation. It was approaching a full year since the FBI punched its Papadopoulos investigation ticket. They had interviewed him. They had accessed his emails. They knew that he had botched his timeline of events. They also had delved into his past. As Mueller would later reveal in his investigative report, his team examined whether Papadopoulos "acted as an agent of, or at the direction and control of, the government of Israel. While the investigation revealed alleged ties between Papadopoulos and Israel (and search warrants were obtained in part on that basis), the Office ultimately determined that the evidence was not sufficient to obtain and sustain a conviction under FARA or Section 951."[16]

Investigators had eight months to dig into all the allegations made in Christopher Steele's FBI reports on Carter Page, Paul Manafort, and Michael Flynn. It was now a race against time for the special counsel. He didn't really think the DOJ inspector general was going to leak anything. That's almost antithetical to what an inspector general does—hold the line and enforce the rules. But this was Washington, D.C., a place that, if it were a ship, would sink faster than a lead *Titanic* thanks to all the backbiters and partisans on both sides of the aisle.

In fact, another leak—actually a leak about an investigation into leaks—further rocked Mueller and Rosenstein's world. On July 27, *Circa* reported that James A. Baker, the FBI's general counsel and Comey's close pal, was under investigation "for allegedly leaking classified national security information to the media."[17] Details about the investigation were scarce—five months later, the *Washington Post* reported he was tied to a "probe of a leak involving the FBI, the National Security Agency and stories that appeared about a year ago involving surveillance techniques for a particular email provider"—and Baker still had not been charged with any wrongdoing. But news that one of the FBI's most respected leaders was under the microscope must have stunned Mueller again. It was starting to look like the upper management staff of his beloved bureau was infected with some kind of sleazy virus.

And yet, despite all this muck and mire, all this deviousness and duplicity, the tenuous evidence, the unverified sources, the raw intelligence that was so dirty you might get contaminated just by reading it, Robert Mueller decided that the investigation was worthy and he would continue to move ahead.

Dumping this sham investigation would have been the standard thing to do. That would be the status quo method. But there were bombshells looming in the future. Scandals that might cripple his team involving Strzok, Page, and Baker. The FBI would have two black eyes and no way to defend itself.

He needed a Plan C. He needed to prove that Christopher Steele's reports—which resulted in the FISA warrant, which he had no idea was a plug-and-play scam—were more fact that fiction. He was going to use the threat of prosecution and the legal heft of the FBI and the special counsel to hit the suspects with charges that would put them between a rock and a hard place known as a federal penitentiary. This was his mindset, I believe. He was going to save the FBI and the DOJ. And he knew exactly how to do it.

He decided to double down on Glenn Simpson and Christopher Steele's plug-and-play reports.

The special counsel determined that the best defense for his beloved FBI was a good offense. Given the circumstances—the facts that Comey had been canned by the president, Strzok had just been exposed, and Baker was under attack—and given Mueller's own long, illustrious background running the bureau, it's really hard to see him playing this any other way. Admitting that the bureau had been tricked into the most controversial, damaging, unnecessary investigation in U.S. history wasn't an option. If he did that, he would have to close the investigation without really nailing anyone. And that was never going to happen. The agency was teetering precipitously, but it wasn't going to collapse on his watch.

He was going to save the FBI by going to war against the Trump campaign.

And if he had to, he was going to go to war against Trump. And it all went down in June and July of 2017.

THE WRIT HITS THE FAN

After months of no visible activity—except leaks and pompous, smug testimony from Comey—the Trump-Russia investigation got busy fast. Rosenstein and Mueller's investigative team started moving in hurry-up offense mode, like the game clock was winding down and they needed to score a few touchdowns. But why the sudden rush?

In the middle of June, George Papadopoulos was approached by an Israeli-American businessman named Charles Tawil. According to Papadopoulos, Tawil bragged to him about doing business with corrupt African presidents and mentioned doing business together. Tawil flew to visit Papadopoulos in Mykonos, Greece. He paid for Papadopoulos to visit Israel for meetings. There, he gave Papadopoulos a suitcase with $10,000 in it, and then paid for Papadopoulos to go to Cyprus. [18]

The entire time, according to Papadopoulos, they had no contract in place. Eventually, Papadopoulos flew to Greece, left the money with a lawyer, and went to meet his future wife in Italy. Remember all this. We'll come back to Papadopoulos in a second.

Early in the morning on July 26, the FBI conducted a shock-and-awe raid on Paul Manafort's home in Alexandria, Virginia. Agents arrived with a search warrant and seized a trove of tax and banking documents. The sudden, unannounced, predawn raid came after investigators had already issued subpoenas to Manafort and his associates demanding details about his income, the *Washington Post* reports.[19] The message from the special counsel was crystal clear: investigators were ratcheting up the pressure on Manafort and they were looking for evidence of financial misdeeds that were not necessarily tied to the campaign investigation.

The *Post* reported the obvious: "Manafort's allies fear that Mueller hopes to build a case against Manafort unrelated to the 2016 campaign, in the hope that he would provide information against others in Trump's inner circle in exchange for lessening his legal exposure."[20]

One day later, July 27, news broke that FBI lawyer James Baker was under investigation. That was the big breaking story in D.C. But something else went down that day. Papadopoulos was greeted by FBI agents at Washington Dulles airport, where they searched his bags repeatedly. According to Papadopoulos's book, the agents appeared very frustrated after going through his bags. Then they arrested him on probable cause without a preapproved warrant.

What were they looking for? Remember, Papadopoulos had been given $10,000—in cash—just weeks before by Charles Tawil, a mysterious businessman who took an interest in Papadopoulos out of the blue. That's a serious amount of cash. If he had been given $9,999 and flown to Dulles airport from Europe, nobody would have blinked. But anyone bringing $10,000 or more in cash into America has to declare it to customs officials. Failing to declare it is a potential crime. If Papadopoulos had trucked in the full amount that Tawil had given him—and Tawil has confirmed giving him the cash—but not declared it, he could have faced possible civil and criminal penalties, including "a fine of not more than $500,000 and imprisonment of not more than ten years, are provided for failure to file a report, filing a report containing a material omission or misstatement, or filing a false or fraudulent report. In addition, the currency or monetary instrument may be subject to seizure and forfeiture."[21]

Luckily for Papadopoulos, he had stashed the cash with a lawyer in Greece. The next day, sleepless, bewildered, and without his lawyers, the former Trump campaign advisor was taken to court. Interestingly, Mueller's dream-team prosecutors showed up late to court. Could it be they were counting on nabbing Papadopoulos on a "failure to report" charge? It seems entirely plausible that they had notified a U.S. attorney about their intentions in a predrafted arrest warrant application, but that any plan to hit Papadopoulos went awry when they discovered Papadopoulos was cashless—and that meant they were forced to scrap their intended charges in favor of an over-the-top probable-cause arrest.

When they did finally arrive in court, they hit Papadopoulos with two charges—neither of which involved collusion. Instead, the man who supposedly kicked off the highest-profile FBI investigation in modern history was accused of lying to an FBI agent and obstructing justice. Both are crimes, and obstruction can carry serious potential jail time. But in Papadopoulos's case, they appear to have been flimsy charges.[22] As he documents in his book, Papadopoulos never had a lawyer present for his initial interview with the two bureau agents. He answered their questions without checking his calendar and email. He got dates and sequences of events wrong regarding Mifsud and his campaign work on meetings that had happened in a whirlwind seven months earlier.[23] Can you remember work meetings from seven months ago off the top of your head? I don't believe we are talking about devious lies here. And, remember, Papadopoulos never denied meeting Mifsud.

The obstruction charge, which carried a maximum sentence of twenty-five years in prison, was even more ridiculous. Papadopoulos had asked his lawyers if he could delete his Facebook account and was advised that he could. So he did. The FBI charged that this was calculated obstruction. Obviously, since Papadopoulos sought advice from counsel, it seems pretty clear he never intended to obstruct anything. He got bad legal advice.

As Papadopoulos himself has noted, his arrest was hardly standard operating procedure for the type of charges he was hit with. As a former law enforcement agent, I can also tell you that nonemergency federal arrests for nonviolent offenders are typically made either in the early morning or during business hours. The reason for that is that the government, prosecutors included, typically work on a nine-to-five schedule. Yes, arrests are made 24/7. But if you are booking someone for a low-key charge, which lying is, you would typically plan it all in advance with the suspect. And when you're trying to induce a nonviolent offender to cooperate in an investigation, making the process as painless as possible for his or her lawyer can be a bonus. Lawmen either set up a time for the suspect to come in and voluntarily turn himself or herself in, or if they're going to hit a house, they do it early in the morning. But staking out Dulles when they knew the subject they were after was flying onward to Chicago? That's not really the definition of a flight risk. I mean, he's coming to America; he's not bolting for the border.

So either Mueller's team had counted on nailing Papadopoulos with the money or they rushed into action, motivated by all the bad mojo surrounding the special investigator, and wanted to change the narrative in a hurry.

Either way, Papadopoulos was given the nastiest, most intimidating treatment possible. He was arrested coming off a plane that arrived in the evening, then he was searched, questioned with hands and legs shackled, processed with a late-night mug shot, thrown into a grim holding cell, and then dragged to his hearing. It's not like he was on the run or a threat. The FBI could have waited for him to get to Chicago, where his lawyers and his family were located. Instead, they went for the airport bust. It seems very likely the FBI knew about the $10,000 in cash—if they were monitoring his phone, they knew he had discussed the cash with his girlfriend and future wife, Simona—and hoped to nail him on an additional charge. So they went for intimidation tactics, trying to terrify the poorest, least-connected, arguably least-experienced person in the entire Trump-Russia investigation into making some kind of admission.

It didn't work. One day later, Papadopoulos was charged, released, and on his way to Chicago, any hopes of landing a job with the Trump administration utterly destroyed.

So in two days, the prosecutors finally made some moves. They decided it was time for their writs to hit the fan, time to flex some muscle and put some pressure on two of Trump's most suspect advisors.

But what did they get out of all of this? Not much when it comes to the collusion investigation.

They got all the Manafort files. All the computer equipment and records taken from the house in Virginia was far more likely to be about his other business interests than about Trump and Russia. They got information about his work with partner Rick Gates, his consulting gigs, his failed real estate ventures, and his previous work for Oleg Deripaska.[24]

But about the Trump campaign and secret deals with Russia? Nothing.

As for the Papadopoulos arrest, FBI agents seemed to have achieved only two things: they both infuriated and scared the hell out of someone on Team Trump. Papadopoulos writes that during the court hearing, he was surprised to hear the prosecutors tell the judge that he was "willing to cooperate with the government in its ongoing investigation into Russian efforts to interfere in the 2016 presidential election." But here's the thing about that: Papadopoulos never colluded or worked with the Russians. So his cooperation wasn't going to help Mueller's mission.

On August 2, 2017, Plan C was officially encoded.

Rod Rosenstein released a second memo redefining the scope of the special investigator probe. It's called "The Scope of Investigation and Definition of Authority." It's four pages long, and nearly half of the publicly released document is redacted. But this section has only one part redacted:

> *The May 17, 2017 order was worded categorically in order to permit its public release without confirm specific investigations involving specific individuals. This memorandum provides a more specific description of your authority. The following allegations were within the scope of the Investigation at the time of your appointment and are within the scope of the Order.*
> *[Redacted]*
> *Allegations that Paul Manafort*
> - *Committed a crime or crimes by colluding with Russian government officials with respect to the Russian government's efforts to intervene with the 2016 election for the President of the United States, in violation of Federal Law.*
> - *Committed a crime or crimes arising out of payments he received from the Ukrainian Government before or during the tenure of President Viktor Yanukovych.*[25]

What was the purpose of this scope memo? Why was it released when it was? For more than a year, I've had two theories on this. The first involves the redacted sections, in which Rosenstein lays out other avenues for Mueller to investigate. I believe this section contains more charges from the reports Steele sent the FBI—which basically echo the dossier. Rosenstein was spelling out instructions in a sort of last-minute Hail Mary pass, hoping Mueller would find somebody who could vindicate the FISA warrant application and save the investigation from being exposed as a megamillion-dollar witch hunt.

The second reason for increasing the scope memo is that Rosenstein wanted to make it crystal clear to Paul Manafort that Robert Mueller had a license to destroy him. Crimes relating to payments from the Ukraine? That could include money laundering, tax evasion, and undeclared income. And there have been numerous stories in the press about this stuff.

With the release of the Mueller report, we now know this is exactly right. He comes clean on page eleven, writing that the August 2 scope memo:

> ...confirmed that the Special Counsel had been authorized since his appointment to investigate allegations that three Trump campaign officials—Carter Page, Paul Manafort, and George Papadopoulos "committed a crime or crimes by colluding with Russian government officials with respect to the Russian government's efforts to interfere with the 2016 presidential election." The memorandum also confirmed the Special Counsel's authority to investigate certain other matters, including two additional sets of allegations involving Manafort (crimes arising from payments he received from the Ukrainian government and crimes arising from his receipt of loans from a bank whose CEO was then seeking a position in the Trump Administration); allegations that Papadopoulos committed a crime or crimes by acting as an unregistered agent of the Israeli government; and four sets of allegations involving Michael Flynn, the former National Security Advisor to President Trump.[26]

Rod Rosenstein released the revised memo to basically underscore his support. He had his own motives for this too, from where I sit. He is the guy who signed off on the fourth FISA warrant application. He essentially underwrote the investigation into a bunch of claims that have basically evaporated or, if not evaporated, have definitely not been confirmed in any way, shape, or form.

At this point in August, the FISA warrant on Carter Page had been open for ten months and renewed four times. Was Page in line for an indictment in August 2017? As I write this now, it's 2019 and he *still* hasn't been indicted. The application Rosenstein signed was based on three ounces of hearsay, two tablespoons of paranoia, a quart of fear, three pounds of misinformation, and a metric ton of politicization. It was a recipe for disaster! The Strzok texts were proof that the whole thing was baseless. The lack of verified allegations was proof it was a fantasy. The fact that there were no emails, texts, or phone calls with Russia or Russian agents that definitively linked Team Trump to an iron-clad conspiracy to steal the election was proof *there was no there there!*

But there *was* proof that Manafort had lied and broken the law. And his own partner, Rick Gates, who had served as the deputy chairman of the Trump campaign, was facing substantial charges, too. There were reports about Manafort's massive debt, about shell companies, and about laundering operations.

So Rosenstein needed to broaden the scope to include targeting Manafort. Manafort was definitely in the Steele reports that had been filed to the FBI and he was mentioned in the dossier. Taking Manafort down would be useful in two ways to Rosenstein and Mueller. First, it would give Mueller's team leverage that could be used to pressure the former campaign chairman to roll on other Trump team members. That would be a huge win because that would prove there was a conspiracy and would justify the entire malevolent operation. Second, even if Manafort didn't talk, nailing him on other charges would still provide him with cover: Manafort was a bad guy. His presence was suspect. Nailing him would prove—at least in Rosenstein's twisted thinking— that the investigation wasn't a corrupt, poorly thought-out extension of a political campaign. It would prove that the FBI hadn't been duped by Simpson and Steele's plug-and-play information-laundering operation.

Rosenstein needed this to prove that everything and everyone who had gone before—the words and deeds of Simpson, Steele, Strzok, Comey, Brennan, and Clapper—were on the up-and-up. That the investigation had been pure of heart and pure of vision. That the FISA warrant application he had signed was legitimate.

The revised scope memo may have had a third purpose, too: to instruct Mueller to investigate obstruction charges. As the Mueller investigation dragged on and on with no surprising indictments or bombshell revelations, I began to suspect that the scope had been broadened to focus on the president himself, and that Mueller and his witch hunters had been fully aware, since the inception of the probe, that the collusion story was a hoax.

But if Rosenstein did instruct Mueller to probe obstruction charges, it would be a truly mind-boggling event. Why? Well, suppose Mueller decided to investigate the Comey firing and treat it as if it were to be part of an obstruction case. Since Trump and Sessions asked Rosenstein to write the memo that justified giving Comey the heave-ho, then the man in charge of the investigation—Rosenstein—would also be a witness to the supposed obstruction—*which should have disqualified him from authorizing the investigation into obstruction.*

Of course, until the entire unredacted scope memo is released, we won't know whom, exactly, it targeted.

PHANTOM PROSECUTIONS

By the end of the summer of 2017, it was obvious that the leads provided by Christopher Steele were never going to lead to a collusion case. The whole thing was a hoax and the investigators knew it. And Andrew Weissmann knew it because he had been briefed by Ohr on the dossier's provenance in August 2016. But was Steele scammed? Was he doing Simpson's dirty work? Were they both abused by Russian countermoves? The answer may be all of the above.

At this point, Rosenstein and Mueller both knew they'd been left holding an empty bag—they'd done all the reading. They'd talked to their team. Mueller's favorite, Weissmann, who led the Manafort portfolio of criminal charges, had examined the source materials. Mueller and Rosenstein had seen the supporting materials. Neither of these guys is stupid. They must have realized that, in terms of actionable evidence, their dream team and the FBI had amassed a donkey cart full of grade-A manure.

Actually, manure is more useful than what these guys found.

So what did they do? What crimes—other than lying to FBI agents, failing to file administrative FARA paperwork, and other process crimes—could they arrest anyone on the Trump team for?

Let's compare a bank robbery investigation to the Russiagate probe. If a bank is robbed and money is taken, there is no question that a crime has been committed. Someone robbed the bank and stole money that did not belong to them. It is law enforcement's job to identify who robbed the bank, to catch the perpetrator, and to recover the money. With Russiagate, investigators thought there might be a crime. But nobody actually dialed 911 and said, "Hey, America is getting ripped off!" No, our own government agencies raised the possibility, apparently after foreign intel agencies and Glenn Simpson, a paid Hillary Clinton operative, sounded the alarm. So our leading law enforcement agency, the FBI, began to investigate. But it couldn't find any hard evidence of a crime beyond Russian cyberoperations and social media interference. The other stuff—allegations of collusion between the Trump campaign and Russia—well, the evidence agents gathered could be filed away wherever they put reports on unicorn sightings.

But for Mueller and Rosenstein, they needed something tangible: the equivalent of a bank robbery. And they didn't have it.

So they stalled.

And they stalled some more.

They were trying to figure out not whether a crime had been committed, but whether they could prove that a crime had been committed. Truth and justice weren't the end game—saving the reputation of the FBI was.

Then, they began to focus on building the only case they could around the only documents that might pass for hard evidence: Comey's

memos documenting his meetings with Trump and the transcripts of
Trump talking about firing Comey.

The special counsel added a new twist to Plan C: launch a case
to bring obstruction-of-justice charges against the sitting president of
the United States—for "obstructing" an investigation into a crime that
never happened.

Of course, the irony of making this move should have been profound
and obvious to Mueller and Rosenstein. The investigation into collusion
was dead. How could Mueller try to nail the president for interfering
with a probe that, from a prosecutorial standpoint, would never result
in collusion charges?

It's absurd. A philosophical conundrum! A kind of legal "If a tree
falls in the forest and nobody heard it, did it make a sound?" question.

Can you obstruct an investigation that shouldn't, when all is said
and done, have been an investigation? An inquiry that arose from a
manufactured plug-and-play operation to destabilize and discredit a
presidential candidate? I'm sure there are plenty of amateur lawyers out
there ready to say that once an investigation is in process, you have to
keep quiet about it. But that's nonsense. What about an investigation
that was essentially a fraudulent political operation or a disinformation
campaign designed to destabilize the United States from within?

In the case of Russiagate, Trump and his campaign were victims,
then. Shouldn't the victim have rights?

I believe the answer to that question, from Robert Mueller's
perspective, was no. It seems he was so eager to damage President
Trump, so horrified by Trump's attack on the swamp, so upset by the
defeat of Hillary Clinton, and so protective of the FBI that surrender
was never an option.

Mueller set his sights on interviewing the president. This was another
Hail Mary pass. The investigation had gone nowhere, and Mueller no
doubt dreamed of tripping up Trump and building a case against him
via a perjury trap. An interminable, predictable jousting match began,

with the president's lawyers refusing to let their client be interviewed and Mueller pressing for access to Trump. The specter of a subpoena to appear before a grand jury loomed in the background, with pundits, legal experts, and Constitution scholars debating the political unknown: could a sitting president even be subpoenaed, let alone indicted? The answer depended on whom was asked.

Meanwhile, on October 3, 2017, the special counsel got a guilty plea deal out of Papadopoulos on charges that he lied to the FBI. The former Trump advisor says he felt forced to do so because the DOJ threatened to file further charges against him for working as an undeclared agent for Israel. It is likely the DOJ was posturing, but Papadopoulos wanted some sort of closure after being harassed for so long.

Then on December 1, 2017, Michael Flynn pled guilty to a similar charge.

As for Paul Manafort, a Virginia jury convicted him on August 21, 2018, of five counts of tax fraud, two counts of bank fraud, and one count of failure to disclose a foreign bank account. Three weeks later, he pled guilty to one count of conspiracy against the U.S. and one count of conspiracy to obstruct justice due to attempts to tamper with witnesses related to illegal Ukrainian lobbying and money laundering.

Also on August 21, Michael Cohen, Trump's morally compromised former lawyer, pled guilty in federal court to violating campaign finance laws and other charges.

Conspicuously absent in all of these pleas and convictions is any mention of the Trump campaign's colluding with Russia to steal the election.

What a surprise.

THE SESSIONS ENDGAME

The entire Russiagate fiasco continued, aimlessly lingering as those behind it refused to state the obvious: that there was no evidence of collusion. Keeping the special counsel investigation open served two needs: it functioned as a huge, potentially lethal open wound in the Trump administration, which gave Trump haters a wild card to wave at every turn, and it allowed Mueller to continue looking for elusive—nonexistent—proof of the crime he initially had been tasked with investigating.

By November 2018, the investigation had gone on for well over two years. It was absurd. Mueller didn't have the nerve or the conviction (or, perhaps, the blessing of Rod Rosenstein) to subpoena Trump, so that legal imbroglio had dissipated. Trump decided the charade had gone on long enough. Rosenstein was overseeing the investigation because Jeff Sessions had foolishly recused himself. If a new attorney general replaced Sessions, the entire power structure behind the investigation—with Rosenstein's protecting his hero Mueller—would come to a crashing halt. On November 7, 2018, after the midterm election with its losses for the Republican Party, Jeff Sessions offered his resignation at Trump's request.[27]

Now Mueller knew his time would soon be up. Whether it would be acting Attorney General Matthew Whitaker or the inevitable full-time attorney general, William Barr, he would have a new boss who could resort to any number of options—from shutting the out-of-control investigation down (which would ignite another political firestorm) to limiting the scope, to demanding that the investigation be wound down. Either way, his time would soon be up.

Mueller and his team focused on Roger Stone, Trump's longtime advisor, whom the anti-Trump cabal had tried to tie to the dumping of hacked DNC emails on WikiLeaks. On January 25, 2019, an unsealed indictment revealed that Stone had been hit with one count of obstruction of an official proceeding, five counts of making false statements, and one count of witness tampering.[28] Stone was the last man taken down by the special counsel in terms of legal action, and as this book was going to press, the outcome of his case was still in limbo.

But Plan C—the mission to save the FBI's reputation and take down Trump—was far from over. Mueller had to issue his findings. And in keeping with everything about Russiagate so far, another round of collusion, coercion, politicization, and bad optics was about to be unleashed.

CHAPTER 7

The Mueller Distortion

When Robert Mueller and his team set about writing up the results and conclusions of the special counsel investigation, he had to face reality.

He and his scheme team had found no hard evidence to confirm nor to prove allegations of collusion between anyone in the Trump campaign and anyone in the Russian government to interfere or influence the 2016 election. This was, for him, an uncomfortable fact.

His investigators had found evidence of process crimes—crimes that were uncovered as a result of the investigation. None of the uncovered violations had anything to do with election interference, and it's likely that most of them would never have surfaced if not for the all-out, take-no-prisoners efforts to discover a crime that didn't exist. Michael Cohen and Paul Manafort are cases in point. They broke the law in a number of ways over a number of years, committing crimes that had nothing to do with election collusion. But they were caught because they were tied to Trump and investigators dug into their past.

Still, unless the charges could make Manafort, Cohen, and others turn state's evidence against the president, they were useless to the Russiagate investigators.

But, again, none of the findings touched Trump. Yes, the president had appointed Flynn his national security advisor and presumably had approved Manafort as his campaign chairman. But he didn't order them to do anything wrong. Still, the unspoken goal of Russiagate, starting with Glenn Simpson's "opposition research," was to expose and hurt Trump's candidacy and, as it turned out, his presidency. And so Robert Mueller began to mull the one charge for which the investigation had amassed evidence. He started building the case against Donald Trump for obstruction of justice.

But there were a number of sticky questions around the obstruction charges. Perhaps the most problematic for Mueller was that Comey, who wrote the memos detailing what he claims were disturbing interactions with Trump, admitted before the Senate that Trump had not actually ordered him to stop the investigation into Michael Flynn when he told Comey: "I hope you can see your way clear to letting this go, to letting Flynn go. He is a good guy. I hope you can let this go."[1]

Republican Idaho senator James Risch clearly established in this exchange with the former FBI director that Trump had not been instructing Comey to drop the charges:

> **Risch**: *Thank you for that. He did direct you to let it go?*
> **Comey**: *Not in his words, no.*
> **Risch**: *He did not order you to let it go?*
> **Comey**: *Again, those words are not an order.*[2]

Of course, Comey later made it clear that he did believe the president had been making his wishes known. Comey said, "I mean, this is a president of the United States with me alone saying I hope this. I took it as, this is what he wants me to do. I didn't obey that, but that's the way I took it."[3]

Mueller was in a tough spot. His key witness, James Comey, seemed to have talked out of both sides of his mouth at the same time. Comey is skilled at that. Comey admitted that Trump had not ordered him to stop the investigation, and yet he said he felt the president had been telling him what to do. As a potential court witness, Comey was going to be pretty easy to twist up thanks to his nuanced double-talk. He was on record as trying to have it both ways.

Mueller had other potential obstruction "evidence" that could be used against Trump, most notably his TV interview with Lester Holt, his remarks to the Russian foreign minister the day after he axed Comey, and his barrage of tweets criticizing the investigation. The Mueller report references the Holt exchange,[4] in which the president downplays the importance of Rosenstein's memo recommending Comey's firing:

> *But regardless of recommendation, I was going to fire Comey knowing there was no good time to do it. And in fact, when I decided to just do it, I said to myself—I said, you know, this Russia thing with Trump and Russia is a made-up story. It's an excuse by the Democrats for having lost an election that they should've won.*[5]

Do any of these "events" prove that Trump had intentionally been trying to interfere with either the FBI probe or, in the case of his tweets, the special counsel's investigation? Good luck with that. The Holt remarks were fundamentally ambiguous, just like his remarks to Comey. The tweets, meanwhile, were just one man's opinion.

It was no secret that Trump was furious with the investigation, and justifiably so. And it is no secret that his working relationship with Comey had been fraught. After all, Comey had lied to the president at Trump Tower in their first meeting by mentioning only the Steele dossier's salacious accusations. The idea that Mueller could use the tweets as obstruction evidence is ludicrous. Regardless of anyone's feelings about Trump, I think we can all agree he is a highly visible, non-focus-group-approved Twitter user. The idea that he would try to obstruct an investigation in full view of the world seems unlikely. But let's give President Trump some credit: I believe he was trying shape public opinion and talk to his base, just as the unethical media leakers investigating a false claim against the president were trying to do. Still, he may have wanted to stop the bleeding from the corrupt investigation, but by doing so in full view, he established plausible deniability.

Add all this up, and Mueller did not have the necessary elements of an obstruction case based on the "evidence" in the public record. No hard-and-fast proof that the president actively or purposefully interfered with the FBI investigation had surfaced.

Mueller may have considered or fantasized that all of these instances of Trump's discussing the investigation would create a preponderance of evidence that might hoodwink a jury into convicting a president. But it is a safe bet that from the moment he took the job of special counsel, Mueller had doubts about ever being able to prosecute a sitting president or an impeached one. He knew this was a legal loser of a case. He knew that many legal experts were on the fence when it came to the constitutionality of indicting a sitting president. And he knew his obstruction case would be dead on arrival in court.

But he appears to have latched on to an interpretation of a particular law, 18 U.S.C. § 1512(c)(2) to drive an obstruction case. Here's the key section of the law that Mueller homed in on:

> (c) Whoever corruptly—
> (1) alters, destroys, mutilates, or conceals a record, document, or other object, or attempts to do so, with the intent to impair the object's integrity or availability for use in an official proceeding; or
> (2) otherwise obstructs, influences or impedes any official proceeding, or attempts to do so [is guilty of the crime of obstruction].[6]

The key phrase here is "or otherwise obstructs."

Will Chamberlain, a lawyer, journalist, and web publisher, has written that Mueller telegraphed his focus on this statute back on January 8, 2018, when his team, requesting an interview with the president, mentioned it had questions about "the president's awareness of and reaction to investigations by the FBI, the House, and the Senate into possible collusion," "the President's reaction to Attorney General Jeff Sessions' recusal from the investigation," and "whether or not [James] Comey's May 3, 2017 testimony led to his termination."

As Chamberlain astutely puts it: "These questions were tells."

In other words, like an amateur poker player, the Mueller team had tipped its collective hand. "None of these questions related to possible collusion by the Trump campaign with the Russian government," Chamberlain writes. "They were all clearly targeted at potential obstruction by the President. And President Trump's legal team knew it."[7]

Since Mueller knew he was on extremely tenuous ground when it came to actually indicting Trump, he knew he needed a shrewd, legally solid defense to file obstruction charges against Trump. Otherwise, even if he did find a magical tape recording or testimony that proved Trump had actively and intentionally tried to undermine and stop the FBI or special counsel from fulfilling its investigatory duty, Trump would likely never stand trial. Section C, then, was his last, best hope. He would have to make a case that the broadly worded statute applied, but apparently he believed it did. Still, he must have known he was on shaky ground.

And in December 2018, he must have felt the earth truly quake. Any doubts he had about bringing charges against Trump were suddenly confirmed. His case was shot.

BARR COMES DOWN

A week after Jeff Sessions submitted his resignation, Donald Trump nominated William Barr as his new attorney general. This would be Barr's second rodeo, so to speak. He had run the DOJ for President George H. W. Bush from 1991 to 1993.

On December 20, 2018, the *Wall Street Journal* broke the news that Barr had sent a memo, prior to his nomination for the attorney general position, to Rod Rosenstein criticizing the Mueller probe's apparent obstruction-of-justice case as "fatally misconceived," in a story titled

"Trump's Attorney General Pick Criticized an Aspect of Mueller Probe in Memo to Justice Department."[8]

Barr sent the twenty-page document to Rosenstein on June 8, the *Journal* reports, noting he was offering his thoughts as a "former official" who hoped his "views may be useful."[9]

Those thoughts, based on reports Barr had read in the media suggesting that Mueller was considering obstruction charges against Trump, attack the very idea that the special counsel would consider questioning the president or charging him with being misguided: "As I understand it, his theory is premised on a novel and legally insupportable reading of the law. Moreover, in my view, if credited by the Justice Department, it would have grave consequences far beyond the immediate confines of this case and would do lasting damage to the Presidency and to the administration of law within the Executive branch."[10]

The memo calls Mueller's approach "grossly irresponsible"[11] and insists that Mueller should not be allowed to force the president to undergo questioning. It continues:

> I know you will agree that, if a DOJ investigation is going to take down a democratically-elected President, it is imperative to the health of our system and to our national cohesion that any claim of wrongdoing is solidly based on evidence of a real crime—not a debatable one. It is time to travel well-worn paths; not to veer into novel, unsettled or contested areas of the law; and not to indulge the fancies by overly-zealous prosecutors."[12]

Ouch.

With that throw-down, Barr lays out his arguments against Mueller, even specifying the conditions he believes would justify a president being charged with obstruction. But Barr notes that the current case Mueller seems to have built doesn't come close to matching the level needed to press his case.

Evidently, Rosenstein was not persuaded by Barr's memo; he certainly didn't appear to curb Mueller's pursuit of the case.

But as of December 2018, once Barr was nominated and his memo was leaked, Mueller knew that any obstruction charges he might propose filing against Trump would never see the light of day. The future head of the Department of Justice—Mueller's soon-to-be-confirmed boss—was dead set against that. And Barr wasn't just objecting to Mueller's actions; he was openly contemptuous of them, using words like "over-zealous," "misguided," and "dangerous."

In other words, Barr's barrage was an accurate assessment.

And when the memo became public, it left Mueller in a bind.

THE FACE-OFF

Mueller, no doubt, vehemently disagreed with Barr. It's easy to imagine he was furious that he couldn't use the scorched-earth tactics honed by his team against the president. There would be no predawn raid on the White House or Trump Tower. No midnight mug shot. Not even a polite question-and-answer session in the Oval Office. No interview, no indictment, no nothing. Game over. His new boss had declared that he believed the case for waging an obstruction investigation of the president was fatally flawed, was unmerited, and would potentially damage the executive branch's ability to set policy and guide the nation.

But that didn't mean Mueller was ready to just give up. He still needed a big win because, as I've theorized here, his ultimate goal, aside from crippling Team Trump, has always been to rescue the reputation of the FBI. And that includes rehabilitating former FBI director James Comey, who, critically, would be the key witness in any obstruction case, as well as the agents who allowed Glenn Simpson, Christopher Steele, and other alarmist Obama and Clinton acolytes to fuel the fabrication of a Russia conspiracy. That's why Mueller followed Christopher Steele's reports—to try to make them come true. And if he couldn't make them come true, he could give them a thin patina of credibility. That's why he went after Manafort so hard—to try to force him to turn on Trump and the rest of the campaign. That's why he spent 675 days searching in vain for any evidence to show that the special counsel investigation was not a frivolous witch hunt and that his beloved FBI, DOJ, and pals working there hadn't been so grossly wrong.

Filing obstruction charges also, on some level, had to be personal. Mueller's own reputation was at stake. Nobody is going to call his investigation write-up "The Special Counsel's Report That Rod Rosenstein Authorized." It has his name on it, unofficially—the Mueller report—and it is having national and international implications. It's the capstone on a career.

So he needed to write a report that would make the investigation look good. Like it had a sliver of integrity. Like the bureau hadn't fallen for something hook, line, and sinker and then leaked a toxic storyline that tore the country in two.

So what did the special counsel do? Robert Mueller decided to go all-in. I believe he thinks that Barr's memo—which is a clear assault on Mueller's reputation and investigation—shows that Barr is out to protect the president at all costs. So he told his team to let it all hang out as they constructed the report. They laid out the "facts" in as negative a light as possible and they left out key exculpatory details. They stressed that the optics had looked awful and that people on Trump's campaign team had behaved in odd ways. That there had been contact between the campaign and Russians. That Manafort had arranged to have polling information sent to "his long-time business associate Konstantin Kilimnik, who the FBI assesses to have ties to Russian intelligence."[13] That Trump had made statements they construed as blurring the line between understandable musing and calculated meddling.

And then, to inflict the most damage of all, they cataloged at least ten instances in which Trump was involved in exchanges that they think could point to obstruction ("could" being the operative word;

logic dictates that these exchanges also could not point to obstruction). Mueller's team also spelled out three issues that are potentially damaging when viewed without context: that Trump's office had provided him with a unique level of influence and power over official proceedings, staff, and potential witnesses; that the evidence pointed to a range of other possible personal motives behind the president's conduct, including "whether certain events…could be seen as criminal activity by the President, his campaign, or his family"; and finally, that "many of the President's acts directed at witnesses, including discouragement of cooperation with the government and suggestions of possible future pardons, occurred in public view."[14]

The Mueller report piles on in numbing detail information about alleged bad behavior, contradictions, appearances, and key dossier figures such as Manafort. You get the sense that the writers hoped the report would become an encyclopedia of embarrassments to the administration and to Barr. I believe Mueller thought that if his team succeeded in presenting an avalanche of "evidence" against Team Trump, then Barr would stop it from being released. For Mueller, that would be a win because the Democrats could then spend the next two years yelling, "Cover-up! Cover-up!" (which Nancy Pelosi predictably began howling in May 2019) and could continue crippling the administration.

But Barr surprised everyone.

First, he decided to release a four-page, topline summary of the report.

In it, Barr ignores the relentless cataloging of Mueller's team. Instead, he gets straight to the basics: the special counsel's report confirmed that the Russian government interfered in the 2016 presidential election, but investigators "did not establish that members of the Trump campaign conspired or coordinated with the Russian government in its election interference activities," he writes.[15] As for obstruction charges, Barr notes that he and Rosenstein have concluded "that the evidence developed during the special counsel's investigation is not sufficient to establish that the President committed an obstruction-of-justice offense. Our determination was made without regard to, and is not based on, the constitutional considerations that surround the indictment and criminal prosecution of a sitting president." But Barr also shares the final, pointed line of the report's conclusion, which I will revisit in a few pages: "While this report does not conclude that the president committed a crime, it also does not exonerate him."[16]

Mueller still refused to go quietly. He sent Barr a letter complaining about the attorney general's summary, a letter he must have known would be leaked to the media. Or rather, it's about the media's interpretation of the summary. He doesn't say Barr got the specific details wrong. Rather, it seems he was upset that the limited overview does "not fully capture the context, nature, and substance" of the full report. Says Mueller:

> There is now public confusion about critical aspects of the results of our investigation. This threatens to undermine a central purpose for which the Department appointed the Special Counsel: to assure full public confidence in the outcome of the investigations.[17]

Mueller's letter to Barr, in keeping with the tactics that defined so much of the probe, was leaked, resulting in a chorus of charges from Democrats accusing Barr of being a Trump apologist who was whitewashing the Mueller report's findings.

Then Barr decided to turn the tables on the special counsel and all the hand-wringing Never Trumpers with a move that was clearly a double-barreled "Up yours" message to all the Russiagate cheerleaders. He did the math and realized that, as harsh as some of the slanted report was, it was better to release it and move on rather than to bury it and have Trump endure a constant barrage of obstruction claims. Can't you just hear all the whining about how Barr was working on Trump's behalf to silence Mueller? To suppress the special counsel's work would have just continued the absurd storylines that had been festering for three years.

So he released the Mueller report.

With minimal redactions.

So the world could now see the "results," such as they were, for themselves.

GASLIGHT NATION

Let me be totally clear where I stand on the Mueller report: it is a 448-page object lesson in gaslighting.[18]

At no point in the two-volume opinion piece disguised as an investigative report does the special counsel address the elephant in the room: whether the foundational, raw intelligence that ignited the investigation was ever fully vetted. There is no mention of the possibility that this intelligence was actually Russian misinformation fed to the FBI or that it was served on a platter to the FBI as the final step in a calculated information-laundering operation by a team hired to provide opposition research for Hillary Clinton. A team, as I have demonstrated in these pages, that was relying on a plug-and-play script to destroy Donald Trump's candidacy and subsequent presidency.

I'm not alone in my feelings about this.

"The dossier is blandly described several times as 'unverified allegations compiled' by Mr. Steele," writes Kimberley Strassel, dissecting the Mueller report for the *Wall Street Journal*.[19]

She goes on:

> *Once Mr. Mueller established that the dossier was a pack of lies, he should have investigated how it gained such currency at the highest levels of the FBI. Yet his report makes clear he had no interest in plumbing the antics of the bureau, which he led from 2001-13. Instead, he went out of his way to avoid the dossier and give cover to the FBI.[20]*

This is not just a conservative viewpoint. Marcy Wheeler, a left-leaning civil liberties journalist who writes the *Empty Wheel* blog and has

admitted that she contributed information to the Mueller investigation about someone she believed was a hostile actor to U.S. interests,
raised the specter of misinformation back on March 6, 2017. Wheeler
speculates that since the DNC hired Simpson, who then hired Steele,
it was entirely possible that Russian intelligence agents learned about
the DNC-Simpson-Steele relationship when they hacked the DNC. If
that's the case, then they knew Steele was working to gather anti-Trump
material. And if they knew that, then they were in the perfect position
to feed him bogus stories.

Also, Steele had been feeding memos on Russia to the State Department since 2009, according to multiple reports. Wheeler and others have
wondered if, over the years, Russia had learned about Steele. Look, I'm
speculating here. So is Strassel. So is Wheeler. Let's be up front: our speculation is informed but *unverified*. Every single raw intelligence report
Steele filed was unverified, too. And in twenty-twenty hindsight, it sure
looks like Steele's speculation was *completely uninformed*. Mueller's
crediting one group of unverified reports but discounting and dismiss-
ing others makes absolutely no sense. Sure, Steele may have helped the
bureau previously. But "unverified" means unverified: nobody knew if
the Trump-Russia information Steele provided was true.

And the warning signs about Steele were everywhere. He couldn't
even keep the basic details of his story straight when he told the State
Department's Kathleen Kavalec, just weeks before the first FISA warrant
was sworn to by the FBI, that the "Russian consulate" in Miami had
played a key role in the collusion scandal. The catch: there *is no* Russian
consulate in Miami. And now it is clear, $35 million of investigatory
legwork later, that the vast majority of those allegations cannot be
proven, likely never happened, and are seemingly part of an active disinformation campaign.

Ironically, when Mueller fired off his brief letter to Attorney General
William Barr on March 27, 2019, taking issue with Barr's four-page
report summary, he couched his complaints in what he tried to spin as

his ultimate mission. Asserting that the public is confused about "critical aspects of" the investigation, he writes: "This threatens to undermine a central purpose for which the Department appointed the special counsel: *to assure full public confidence in the outcome of the investigations.*"[21] (Emphasis added.)

Excuse me?

How can the public have confidence in the investigations if Mueller and his report fail to delve into the underlying intelligence that was used to justify the entire probe? Remember that the very first sentence of Rod Rosenstein's scope memo says Mueller had been appointed "to ensure a full and thorough investigation of the Russian government's efforts to interfere in the 2016 presidential election."[22] Mueller is happy to share the evidence when it comes to Russian hacking and cyberinfluencing campaigns. When it comes to discovering the source of Christopher Steele's raw intelligence? Total silence.

The truth is, the FBI dropped the ball when it came to vetting intel. And Mueller refused to charge it with an error, despite spending 675 days trying to prove that relying on Glenn Simpson and Christopher Steele's research wasn't a mistake. Then he compounded the error by never, at least according to what's included in the report, vetting Steele or identifying the informants.

But the biggest error, the biggest breach, the biggest failure of the Mueller report is that it ultimately failed to deliver on its mandate. It got convictions. It found ancillary wrongdoing and crimes by some Trump campaign associates. But it did not find collusion. And this is what really confounds me, because I know Robert Mueller has dedicated his life to public service—from his tour as a Marine platoon commander in Vietnam to his years with the DOJ and FBI. If his team did find obstruction evidence, shouldn't Mueller have had the guts to file the charge he so clearly wanted to?

Maybe, as I've just explained, it's because he knew on some level he had to adapt the instructions of the scope memos that defined his mission in order to protect his other mission: rescuing the FBI and protecting the bureau from further embarrassment.

I'm going to return to Mueller's conclusion, which I mentioned a few pages back, so you can see what I'm talking about. Then we'll get back to gaslighting. Here is the last page of the Mueller report. It is a master class in waffling, in speaking out of both sides of your mouth. In damning without indicting. In branding without owning. It's the ultimate in casting aspersions. Here:

IV. Conclusion

Because we determined not to make a traditional prosecutorial judgment, we did not draw ultimate conclusions about the President's conduct. The evidence we obtained about the President's actions and intent presents difficult issues that would need to be resolved if we were making a traditional prosecutorial judgment. At the same time, if we had confidence after a thorough investigation of the facts that the President clearly did not commit obstruction of justice, we would so state. Based on the facts and the applicable legal standards, we are unable to reach that judgment. Accordingly, while this report does not conclude that the President committed a crime, it also does not exonerate him.[23]

This a staggering piece of legalese. It appears to pass the buck while also passing judgment. If the "report does not conclude that the President committed a crime," then doesn't it conclude that the president did not commit a crime? That would stand to reason, right? But no, Mueller, the crack logician, is splitting hairs. After 675 days of hectoring and analyzing, he couldn't make a call. Instead he blamed the nonconclusion on DOJ policy—"the applicable legal standards" and the facts.

I love that he cites "facts." Generally, when facts prove a case, they usually result in a guilty verdict. When facts conflict or are inconclusive, they often result in an acquittal.

What does a jury say when it decides to acquit a defendant?

It says the defendant is—repeat after me, Robert Mueller—"not guilty"!

There was no real trial by a jury here, obviously. But Mueller, in his private deliberations with his scheme team, weighed the evidence and realized that even if Attorney General Barr would allow the DOJ to press a case, it didn't have enough hard evidence of intent to ensure a conviction. So Mueller punted.

What a cop-out!

One of the shrewd aspects of taking this position is that Mueller also says he has no opinion. And then he offers one in the last sentence, claiming the report does not exonerate Donald Trump.

I was apoplectic when I read that last paragraph. I still am.

There's no conclusive evidence of wrongdoing, at least not enough for Mueller to put his reputation on the line. There's no evidence of collusion or working with Russia. And 675 days have dragged on with no subpoena or indictment of Trump. And now, in the entire 448-page document, there is no conclusive proof that Trump broke the law.

And yet the special counsel insists that Trump is not exonerated?

Did I wonder about Mueller's guts? Now I have to wonder about his intellect. This conclusion shows he has a hell of a lot of nerve but not a lot of smarts. I get what Mueller is trying to do here. He wants to thread the needle and say, "I can't prove Trump is guilty, but I'm not going to say he's innocent, either."

In the end, Mueller does seem to offer up a verdict and a recommendation, suggesting that Congress impeach Trump if it believes the president engaged in "corrupt use of his authority": "With respect to whether the president can be found to have obstructed justice by exercising his powers under Article II of the Constitution, we concluded that Congress has authority to prohibit a President's corrupt use of his authority in order to protect the integrity of the administration of justice."[24]

By pointing out that the president has a "constitutional duty to faithfully execute the laws"—no kidding!—Mueller implies that Trump hasn't been doing that. Then he notes that Congress is mandated "to protect official proceedings, including those of courts and grand juries, from corrupt, obstructive acts regardless of their source."[25]

And that leads to him handing off the case to Capitol Hill on a platter: "The conclusion that Congress may apply the obstruction laws to the President's corrupt exercise of the powers of the office accords with our constitutional system of checks and balances and the principle that no person is above the law."[26]

Let me translate that: "I've just laid out what I think Trump did, but Barr won't let me pursue these charges. Since I am a professional who talks about rule of law, I'm not going to challenge Barr. Instead, I'm going to punt this over to Congress and, in plain sight, remind them that they can impeach the president."

How does that ensure respect for the integrity of the process that Mueller stated was the whole purpose of his probe? As the second-to-last sentence of the initial scope memo says: "If the Special Counsel believes it is necessary and appropriate, the Special Counsel is authorized to prosecute federal crimes arising from the investigation of these matters."[27] It doesn't say that "the Special Counsel is authorized to pass the buck to Congress and let Congress politicize the matter for another two years"! But that is what Mueller has done. I believe he knew that facing off against Barr would end badly and that a trial, much less a conviction at a trial, would be impossible, so he decided to prolong the distrust and the crippling narrative by pointedly advising Congress to do the same. What a guy.

SINS OF OMISSION, PART ONE

The Mueller report also contains numerous sloppy, contradictory, and cloudy sections, and it frequently confounds logic. But zoom in on some of the most egregious and alarming issues and you'll see that the report is more disturbing for what it doesn't say than for what it says.

Let's take the mysterious case of Joseph Mifsud, the Maltese professor with ties to Western intelligence officials who tried to inject a collusion storyline into the campaign by telling George Papadopoulos that the Russians had "dirt" on Clinton. "'Emails of Clinton,' he says. 'They have thousands of emails,'" is how Papadopoulos remembers the claim.[28]

There is no available evidence proving Mifsud was, or is, a Russian spy. But the Mueller report describes him as having "Russian contacts." Then it lists his connections to Russians with ties to Russian cyberintelligence.[29]

But nowhere does it note that Mifsud also has deep political connections to liberal Italian politicians; that he posed for photos with British politician Boris Johnson, who served as England's foreign minister; that he was frequently seen in the European Parliament; or that he was hanging out with Italian Socialist and Democratic Party leader Gianni Pittella. Mifsud has posed with so many Western politicians and diplomats that the BBC once called him the "selfie king of the diplomatic circuit."[30]

The report also fails to note that Mifsud's own lawyer has published a book in which he says that Mifsud has far more ties to Western intelligence and politicians than to Eastern European ones, basically disavowing the notion that he was working for the Russians.[31] Finally, at no point does anyone raise what seems like an obvious question: did Papadopoulos, who was spun left and right by at least four operatives, all asking him leading questions about Russia, simply misremember his exchange with Mifsud? Or did others mischaracterize what Papadopoulos had said? Is this, in other words, a giant transcontinental game of telephone in which the evidence evolved over time, as the principal subjects and investigators batted whispered allegations about "dirt" and "emails" back and forth?

As Andrew McCarthy astutely points out in *The National Review*, Australian high commissioner Alexander Downer, the primary source who flagged Papadopoulos to the FBI, propelled the probe forward with what he thought he had heard:

> *Mueller carefully describes not what Papadopoulos said to Downer, but what Downer understood Papadopoulos had "suggested," namely that "the Trump Campaign had received indications from the Russian government that it could assist the Campaign through the anonymous release of information that would be damaging to Hillary Clinton."*[32]

Casting even more doubt on the whole "sky is falling" Russia-Clinton alleged email crisis are two other notable issues. First, Maltese mystery man Mifsud was interviewed by the FBI in February 2017, and he denied mentioning or knowing about the Clinton emails.[33] Second, if he had known about the emails, he would have been wrong—since Russian agents allegedly hacked the DNC emails, not Clinton's or her campaign's. So, again, shouldn't the special counsel have at least entertained the possibility that Papadopoulos may have had a faulty memory?

Given all this—plus the fact that Mifsud utterly failed to provide Papadopoulos with any significant Kremlin contacts to set up a possible meeting with candidate Trump—there is plenty of conflicting evidence here. But in his report, Mueller opts to withhold any evidence that might upend the narrative the FBI had bought—or possibly helped create— three years before and continued to feed to the American public.

In the end, however, the report is forced to nearly exonerate Papadopoulos: "No documentary evidence, and nothing in the email accounts or other communications facilities reviewed by the Office, shows that Papadopoulos shared this information with the Campaign."[34]

But that didn't stop the FBI and special counsel from going crazy trying to prove otherwise: that Mifsud was a Russian agent and Papadopoulos was some kind of colluding traitor. For shame.

One last thing about the report's obvious and curious omissions regarding Papadopoulos: nowhere in the report is there a single mention of Stefan Halper or his "research assistant" Azra Turk, the operatives sent at Papadopoulos by the FBI and who exchanged emails with him. It is, as writer Paul Sperry notes, "Another example of how Mueller's probe was really designed to protect the FBI/DOJ."[35]

Speaking of Halper, there is no mention of him at all in the Mueller report. This is a truly shocking omission. A lifelong operative, Halper himself was so entrenched in spycraft and networking that he was beyond a liability. Never mind that Papadopoulos almost instantly made him for a spy; it is starting to look as if Halper may have had more connections to Russian espionage masters than anyone in this whole fiasco.

As Sara Carter reported in August 2018, while Halper was running the Cambridge Intelligence Seminar at the University of Cambridge, he "invited senior Russian intelligence officials to co-teach his course on several occasions and, according to news reports, also accepted money to finance the course from a top Russian oligarch with ties to Putin."

Course syllabi reveal that one man who shared the course load with Halper in 2012 and 2015 is former director of Russian intelligence Chief Vyacheslav Trubnikov. Carter also notes that the British press also reported, "Halper received funds for the Cambridge seminar from Russian billionaire Andrey Cheglakov, who has close ties to Russian President Vladimir Putin."

None of this is mentioned in the gaslighting document of the century.

The Mueller report doesn't care if Halper has direct contacts to Russian intelligence. It should have cared, and I'm about to tell you why, but get ready for a mind-boggling detour that casts even more shadows on Christopher Steele and James Comey. Not that we need actually need any more evidence against them at this point.

Let's go back to October 11, 2016, when Assistant Secretary of State Kathleen Kavalec met with Christopher Steele and listened to a breathless version of his fiction-filled intel. She took notes and wrote up a memo on the exchange. In it, she noted that Steele had told her that the "institution" employing him was "keen to see this information come to light prior to November 8." This is a stunning admission. It makes clear that the DNC and the Clinton campaign wanted Steele's unvetted allegations to help influence the presidential race.[36]

At one point in the summary, Kavalec describes what Steele's "sources" had told him:

> There is technical/human operation run out of Moscow targeting the election. There is a significant Russian network in the U.S. run by the Russian Embassy that draws on emigres to do hacking and recruiting.... Payments are made out of the Russian Consulate in Miami."[37]

Kavalec then inserts her own editorial comment in the write-up: "It is important to note that there is no Russian Consulate in Miami." In other words, she had quickly realized that at least one detail in Steele's "intel" was completely off the mark—a point that should have raised flags for anyone vetting Steele's raw intelligence.[38]

How did the FBI miss this stuff? How did Mueller miss it—or did he just choose to omit it from his report?

There's at least one more highly damning revelation in Kavalec's write-up. Her handwritten notes taken while Steele was talking were also saved. The notes are scattershot, but one page makes references to "sources" and "sourcing," and there is a hard-to-read name in her notes.[39] A law enforcement contact of mine studied the document and deciphered the enigmatic scrawl. His conclusion?

Trubnikov—the Russian spymaster who worked with Halper.

My contact wasn't alone, either: reporter Chuck Ross decoded the scribble with the same result.[40]

This suggests that Steele, at some point, mentioned the former director of Russian intelligence to Kavalec. Was he Steele's source? Why else would the name surface? And if that's the case, well, then Steele was using information from a known Russian espionage leader and feeding it to the FBI. This is the real Russia-collusion story: it seems more and more likely that Steele's information was Russian misinformation.

And this again leads us back to Halper, the operative who turns up in so many places in this story. Was he driving sources to Steele? Was he fabricating tales as he appeared to do regarding Michael Flynn and a so-called Russian honeytrap, and as he definitely did while trying to con George Papadopoulos? Aren't any of this man's dubious dealings worth exposing? How could the FBI work with someone so potentially compromised, someone who, according to Papadopoulos, was a completely charmless bully?

That Steele and Halper both seem to have connections to Trubnikov should have cast further doubt on the dossier's allegations. That it didn't, and that the Mueller report mentions none of this, just makes the gaslighting even more apparent.

Not surprisingly, the names of Peter Strzok and Lisa Page, the disgraced FBI agent and lawyer, are also missing from the Mueller report. So is the name Josh Pitcock.

On June 29, 2017, the *New York Times* reported that Pitcock would leave his job as Vice President Mike Pence's chief of staff. It now appears that his departure may have been initiated by the discovery of texts between Strzok and Page that indicate Pitcock was being targeted by the FBI. An April 25, 2019, letter by Senators Chuck Grassley and Ron Johnson to William Barr lays out the issue:

> *In text messages exchanged between former FBI Special Agent Peter Strzok and former FBI Attorney Lisa Page, the two discussed the possibility of developing "potential relationships" at a November 2016 FBI briefing for presidential transition team staff.*[41]

In their exchange, the devious duo discuss which "CI guy"—which presumably means "counterintelligence guy"—should attend a transition team briefing with William Evanina, the director of the National Counterintelligence and Security Center. Here's the end of the exchange.

Keep in mind that, while the identity of Charlie is unknown, Katie is likely Katherine Seaman, the wife of Josh Pitcock, who worked as an FBI counterintelligence analyst; Joe is likely FBI agent Joe Pientka; Andy is likely FBI bigwig McCabe; and Bill is probably FBI deputy counterintelligence director Bill Priestap:

> *Strzok: Talking with Bill. Do we want Joe to go with Evanina instead of Charlie for a variety of reasons?*
>
> *Page: Hmm. Not sure. Would it be unusual to have [sic] show up again? Maybe another agent from the team?*
>
> *Strzok: Or, he's "the CI guy." Same.might [sic] make sense. He can assess if there are [sic] any news [sic] Qs, or different demeanor. If Katie's husband is there, he can see if there are people we can develop for potential relationships*
>
> *Page: Should I ask Andy about it? Or Bill want to [sic] reach out for andy [sic]?*
>
> *Strzok: I told him I'm sure we could ask you to make the swap if we thought it was smart. It's not until Mon so Bill can always discuss with him tomorrow.*[42]

What does this mean? It appears that the FBI was discussing placing a mole at the Trump team briefing and potentially having Pitcock help identify future recruits for its counterintelligence investigation.

In other words, the FBI was looking to infiltrate the transition team.

There is no evidence that Pitcock actually helped these guys out. But these texts sure make it seem like the FBI expected him to cooperate as the bureau spied on the incoming administration. Additionally, these texts again show the desperate, craven lengths to which the FBI was ready to go to try to nail Trump. So again, it's no surprise that Mueller makes no mention of them in his report.

The infamous June 9 Trump Tower meeting in Donald Trump Jr.'s office is also detailed in the Mueller report. This is the meeting in which Russian lawyer Natalia Veselnitskaya met Trump Jr., Paul Manafort, and Jared Kushner. It was set up by publicist Rob Goldstone, who pitched

Trump Jr. that "the Crown prosecutor of Russia" (note: no such position exists) and Veselnitskaya, a connected Russian lawyer, had "very high level and sensitive information" that could damage the Clinton campaign.[43] Trump Jr. responded that "if it's what you say I love it especially later in the summer."[44] The anti-Trump witch hunters have suggested this was collusive behavior, embracing damning revelations coming from a foreign government or source. But how is that any different than, say, receiving a dossier from a former British intelligence operative working on "opposition research" who claims to have former high-level Russian intelligence figures as "sources"?

The Mueller report gives a thirteen-page play-by-play of the Trump Tower meeting. It also gives a thorough biography of Veselnitskaya. There are some redactions of the text in this section, but nowhere does it appear to mention that Veselnitskaya met with Glenn Simpson—the DNC and Clinton campaign operative who hired Christopher Steele to write the Trump-damaging dossier—for dinner both the night before and the night after the Trump Tower meeting. Why did they meet? Because Simpson and his company, Fusion GPS, were also working for Veselnitskaya. Simpson has claimed that he was unaware his Russian client had a meeting scheduled with the son of the Republican Party nominee for president. To me, this means that Veselnitskaya is a world-class poker player, that Simpson has severe memory issues, or that Simpson is lying.

Remember, by June 9, Simpson had likely already engaged Steele—given that he told the Senate Judiciary Committee he hired Steele in "May or June"[45]—to gather intel on Team Trump. In the coming weeks, Steele would meet with Bruce Ohr and begin filing memos based on the dossier that alleges that Paul Manafort and Carter Page had secret meetings with Russian sources. The Trump Tower meeting appears, on the surface, to possibly corroborate those claims. It stands to reason that Simpson hoped and suspected that the FBI was, or would be, investigating whether Team Trump members were meeting with Russians—because that is the story Steele fed them. The Trump Tower June 9 meeting, then, could have been waved around as evidence. And that's exactly how it was portrayed in the mainstream media. Once again, it provided the *impression* of possible wrongdoing.

But if you want to talk about impressions, the connections between Simpson and Veselnitskaya and between Simpson and Steele seem much more damning. Veselnitskaya, a Russian with connections to Russian intelligence, met with the Trump team and then one month later, Steele filed reports about the Trump team's meeting with the Russians. Isn't that suspicious?

Not, apparently, if you are the special counsel.

There was one other Trump Tower meeting attendee with a strange set of connections that the Mueller report conveniently ignores: Rinat Akhmetshin, an alleged Russian-intelligence-connected lobbyist who was working with Veselnitskaya on behalf of Prevezon Holdings in an effort challenge the Magnitsky Act—the U.S. law blacklisting Russian human rights abusers—and trying to gain access to millions of dollars in Prevezon funds frozen by the U.S. government under the statute. While Akhmetshin's alleged spy background seems to have been an ideal collusion conduit for Team Trump and the Russians, the initial impression appears to have been far from the actual truth. Appearing before the Senate Judiciary Committee on November 14, 2017, he denied working in Russian counterintelligence and he shared his dislike of Trump—"I'm not a fan of the whole family"—and revealed that he had met Hillary Clinton in social settings and "knew some people who worked on her campaign." He had plenty of other close connections to the candidate through his lawyer.[46]

None of Akhmetshin's Clinton connections or scorn for Trump are mentioned in the report's rundown of the June 9 meeting. And that seems highly ironic: everyone made such a huge deal about Veselnitskaya having ties to Russia's chief prosecutor and turning up at Trump Tower, but nobody gave a damn that a Clinton crony was sitting there too, listening to the team members discussing his acquaintance! The double standard is absurd.

In the end, however, the Mueller report concludes that the Trump Tower meeting was much ado about nothing. All records relating to the meeting—including interviews, emails, and texts—show that no meaningful or damaging information about Hillary Clinton was exchanged. Mueller's report also leaves out the myriad of connections between Konstantin Kilimnik and President Barack Obama's State Department, where he served as a source of intelligence information. Who is Kilimnik, you ask? He's the Paul Manafort associate whose frequent interactions with Manafort, and suspected Russian connections, are painted as nefarious in the Mueller report.

Once again, what appeared to be a fire was only smoke.

Speaking of illusions—or maybe I mean delusions—guess how many pages of the Mueller report contain the name Christopher Steele?

Nine.

Guess how many pages of the Mueller report evaluate the information that Christopher Steele provided to the FBI and in his well-publicized dossier?

Zero.

This is a truly fascinating omission. The man who provided the primary "evidence" used to obtain the FISA warrant and drive the entire Mueller investigation is barely mentioned in the investigation's final report. This is Steele's biggest cameo in the entire 448-page document:

> *Several days later, BuzzFeed published unverified allegations compiled by former British intelligence officer Christopher Steele during the campaign about candidate Trump's Russia connections under the headline "These Reports Allege Trump Has Deep Ties To Russia."*[47]

Pretty much every other mention of Steele in the report is made in passing with a brief mention of the dossier. There is no exhumation, no analysis, and no detail about the credibility of Steele's FBI reports or his dossier.

There is also no mention of Glenn Simpson or Simpson's firm Fusion GPS in the special counsel's write-up. The man who I believe did more than anyone else to drive the Trump-Russia collusion story forward, the man who knew Manafort was dirty, the man who knew there was a script to follow and then directed it from the shadows—hiring Steele, unleashing him on the world, talking to DOJ officials and his journalist pals—does not substantively exist in the entire special counsel narrative.

Think about that for a while.

Once your outrage subsides, ask yourself what this absence means. Why has Glenn Simpson been airbrushed out of these events? Why is Christopher Steele nothing more than a passing figure?

Because digging into Simpson and Steele's work, as I have shown here, would mean digging into a series of politicized lies. And that would expose the FBI management cabal running the Trump investigation, the organization Mueller devoted so much of his life to, as a politically motivated group of swamp rats abusing their power. It would also expose the U.S. intelligence leaders under the Obama administration as politicized incompetents.

And that was not Mueller and Rosenstein's game. The special counsel was on a rescue mission. And the report was and is part and parcel of that mission.

Thirty-five million dollars, 675 days, and 448 pages later, America still doesn't know whether Christopher Steele was fed misinformation by Russian intelligence.

Thirty-five million dollars, 675 days, and 448 pages later, America still doesn't know for certain the real reason the FBI relied so heavily on a discredited Christopher Steele's information to advance the biggest hoax in American history.

Thirty-five million dollars, 675 days, and 448 pages later, America still doesn't know if what Simpson's wife implied on Facebook is true— that he directed Steele in compiling the dossier.

Thirty-five million dollars, 675 days, and 448 pages later, America has no idea whether the Steele dossier was the creation of Vladimir Putin's counterintelligence division. All we know is that the raw information in the dossier that was fed to the FBI was almost all completely wrong and politically toxic.

SINS OF OMISSION, PART TWO

So much has been left out of the Mueller report that it is exhausting to document. But let me add a few more inconvenient truths that the legal sages knowingly skirted around. They are important because they reveal the full extent of the Mueller team's efforts to foist a biased report on the public.

The investigators devote a lengthy section of their wrap-up to Michael Cohen's testimony to Congress. As the world now knows, Cohen, who was also convicted of tax fraud, making false statements to a bank, and campaign finance violations, pled guilty to lying to Congress on November 29, 2018, saying he "made these statements to be consistent with" Trump's "political messaging and out of loyalty to Trump."[48]

When Cohen made those false statements, according to the Mueller report, he "understood Congress's interest in him to be focused on the allegations in the Steele reporting concerning a meeting Cohen allegedly had with Russian officials in Prague during the campaign."[49]

We know that Steele's truly alarming allegation about Prague—his claim that Trump sent Cohen to pay off Russian hackers—was false because Cohen had never traveled to Prague. But the report just ignores the Steele dossier's fabricated claim of Trump collusion as if it were some tiny detail, mentioning the Czech Republic capital twice on a single page and essentially breezing over yet another false report from Steele.[50] But this isn't some trifling charge; it is a huge and frightening allegation that merges fact—the Russians were using hackers and cyberwarfare to influence the election—with the damaging fiction that Trump was colluding and funding the operation. Again, the Mueller team's report makes a conscious effort to steer clear of the poisonous "information" that led to the entire investigation.

One last thing on the Cohen section: I want to stress how the authors take pains to prosecute Trump in print.

Before going over Cohen's version of events in slow-mo, the Mueller report confirms that investigators found *no* evidence that Trump directly influenced or tried to influence Cohen's congressional fibs.

> With regard to Cohen's false statements to Congress, while there is evidence, described below, that the President knew Cohen provided false testimony to Congress about the Trump Tower Moscow project, the evidence available to us does not establish that the President directed or aided Cohen's false testimony.[51]

Despite this conclusion, the report then delivers a forensic analysis of Cohen and Trump's interactions and possible motivations. Even though the authors have just noted that nothing proves that Trump directed Cohen's testimony, they go on to imply the exact opposite:

> ...there is evidence that could support the inference that the President intended to discourage Cohen from cooperating with the government because Cohen's information would shed adverse light on the President's campaign-period conduct and statements.[52]

This is one of the many times the authors convey wrongdoing on Trump's part without convicting or even accusing him of anything. It is another example of calculated character assassination.

Another major player in Russiagate, WikiLeaks, also goes under the microscope in the report. As has been widely documented, the controversial site published a huge trove of documents from the Democratic Congressional Campaign Committee and the Democratic National Committee that were, the report concludes, stolen by the GRU, Russia's military intelligence agency. And early in the report, investigators state that Trump and the campaign "showed interest in WikiLeaks's releases of documents and welcomed their potential to damage candidate Clinton."[53] Republican Florida congressman Matt Gaetz, however, got to the heart of the bogus collusion narrative during a TV interview on April 18, 2019, while discussing the Mueller report:

> *No evidence is cited, however, showing WikiLeaks knew the GRU was behind the hacks. Or that the Trump team knew the Russians were behind the hack. WikiLeaks detested Hillary Clinton. Trump was facing Hillary Clinton in the presidential race.*
>
> *Just because two ships are both sailing in the same direction, it doesn't mean they've agreed with one another to chart the same course. So here you got a circumstance where obviously Donald Trump Jr. wanted bad information about Hillary Clinton to be in the public sphere. Russia wanted the same thing. But there was no agreement for them to coordinate or collude or conspire to make that happen. That's why we're unable to charge Donald Trump Jr.*
>
> *If there was a meeting of the minds, if there was evidence to support those claims, then I think you would have seen a criminal indictment. But obviously, the people who wrote this report are no fans of the president. You had Andrew Weissmann, who was a Hillary Clinton booster. You had Jeannie Rhee, who represented the Clinton Foundation against FOIA requests.*
>
> *So this was a group of people who had an ax to grind. And though they couldn't bring charges because they didn't want to be—they couldn't sustain them, they still wrote that stuff.*[54]

Gaetz got that 100 percent right. At the end of the day, despite certain commonalities, there is no evidence that WikiLeaks knew the source of the documents was the GRU or that Putin's people were stirring the pot. And there is no evidence that Trump's team knew the Russians had provided the documents to WikiLeaks.

Conspiracy requires knowing the intent of others. While the writers of the report located communications from WikiLeaks personnel that make it clear that the organization wanted to cause Clinton harm, there is no direct line showing that WikiLeaks or the Trump campaign knew that Russia was behind the document dump.

So what the report omits here is that the actions of three separate organizations were conflated by Christopher Steele and his dossier "sources" into one sinister, nonexistent conspiracy. And the FBI and the special counsel spent countless hours and cash running down this conflation and then refused to state the obvious: that distinct events and organizations had been accused of working together without any proof that they were. That conclusion is conveniently missing from the Mueller report.

As I stated earlier, Russiagate and the resulting Mueller report owe their existence to a number of events: Glenn Simpson's 2007 article and the subsequent plug-and-play anti-Trump operation; the politicized cesspool of the Obama administration; the firing of James Comey; and the fact that Trump was turning the status quo on its head. But perhaps no single event allowed Russiagate to spiral out of control more than Jeff Sessions's decision to recuse himself from any and all investigations involving Russia and the Trump campaign.

His punting the responsibility to Rod Rosenstein resulted in the appointment of Mueller and the sliced-and-diced 448-page document that omits key exculpatory evidence for Trump.

The report's authors delve into the actions that led to Sessions's recusal—although they harness it to recount how the announcement of the special counsel led a despondent Trump to rant at his attorney general about how an investigation might cripple his administration. Still, Sessions comes out of the report looking like a wronged man, not so much by the president but by the media and investigators who could have cleared the air of collusion fears.

> With respect to Sessions' statements that he did "not recall any discussions with the Russian Ambassador...regarding the political campaign" and he had not been in contact with any Russian official "about the 2016 election," the evidence concerning the nature of Sessions' interactions

with Kislyak makes it plausible that Sessions did not recall discussing the campaign with Kislyak at the time of his statements. Similarly, while Sessions stated in his January 2017 oral testimony that he "did not have communications with Russians," he did so in response to a question that had linked such communications to an alleged "continuing exchange of information" between the Trump Campaign and Russian government intermediaries. Sessions later explained to the Senate and to the Office that he understood the question as narrowly calling for disclosure of interactions with Russians that involved the exchange of campaign information, as distinguished from more routine contacts with Russian nationals. Given the context in which the question was asked, that understanding is plausible.[55]

And yet no mention is made of the firestorm of weaponized leaks and charges that forced Sessions to adopt his hands-off approach. The Never Trump outcry created a high-profile scandal where none should have ever existed. The Mueller report often supplies context when it wants to damn Trump or a campaign member. But in addressing the sequence of events behind the tarring and feathering of Jeff Sessions, very little context is applied beyond the reality of whether or not he lied about his contacts with Russians. The report concludes it is "plausible" he did not. It doesn't mention a damn thing about all those who accused Sessions of lying, or why they wanted to taint him with the idea that he was hiding something about his relationship with Russia. Why is all that missing? Because examining the motives behind damaging Sessions would draw a direct line from a politicized anti-Trump movement to the creation of the special counsel's investigation, the efforts to investigate obstruction charges and, ultimately, the report itself.

No wonder Mueller didn't provide context!

I could go on identifying the gaslighting, the rewriting, the hypocritical and selective use of evidence and facts, and the lack of context in page after page of the special counsel's report. But the ultimate takeaway is that what Attorney General William Barr wrote in his four-page overview of the report was 100 percent true. Despite their relentless cataloging of selective events, miscast intents, and blurry optics, the investigators "c."[56] And "the evidence developed during the Special Counsel's investigation is not sufficient to establish that the President committed an obstruction-of-justice offense."[57]

In other words, Mueller's claim notwithstanding, the president has been completely exonerated.

CHAPTER 8

The Deep State Sails to Ukraine

I want to return to Representative Matt Gaetz's metaphor of two ships traveling in the same direction. So much of Russiagate involved investigators and Never Trumpers trying to force a connection between events when none truly existed. There was, as Gaetz says, "no meeting of the minds."[1] But let's strip down that metaphor and use it to pose another question. What about tracking a ship—a giant yacht, really—that was traveling solo and picked up passengers who were all pals, who shared a common interest in self-dealing and keeping control of the power they had amassed? And what if, on that journey, they decided to stop at a specific destination where they could arrange deals that would help them arrive at their final destination: in power in Washington, D.C.—what would you call that?

A conspiracy?

The particular luxury yacht cruise I'm talking about concerns a vessel known as the Obama administration, and the stopover is Ukraine, a place awash in dirty money, political infighting, and the shadows of not just Russian influence but American influence as well.

And who was at the heart of this influence, the captain of this cash-happy cruise? It was Joseph Biden, the vice president of the United States and the former colleague of Trump's election rival, Hillary Clinton.

Okay, let's sink this ship metaphor and get down to the facts. Documented reporting shows that Joe Biden's son Hunter had extensive professional and monetary ties to Burisma Holdings, a Ukrainian energy company that was under investigation in Ukraine for improper foreign transfers of money. It also shows that U.S. officials pressured Ukrainian diplomats to change prosecutors looking into the case.[2]

When those entreaties proved fruitless, Daddy Biden stepped in—but not until Hunter's clients got their money back.

This twisted tale also involves a Clinton Foundation payoff and efforts to set up Paul Manafort. More than anything, it highlights the moral bankruptcy of Joe Biden, a guy whose unctuous, oozing smile masks the identity of a profiteering swamp creature—a guy who engaged in two disgusting big-money arrangements that reek of quid pro quo.

The story starts in February 2014, when Ukraine president Viktor Yanukovych's decision not to join the European Union detonated a popular uprising in Kiev. Yanukovych, who had long had the backing of Putin, was forced to flee to Russia. Moscow moved troops into the Crimea region of Ukraine, resulting in an immediate international outcry. As the Ukrainian crisis unfolded, Obama designated Biden as his point man in the area. On February 24, 2014, Obama revealed that his vice president had been dispatched to tell the Ukrainian prime minister that the U.S. fully supported the former Soviet nation's sovereignty.

Three months later, on May 12, 2014, Burisma Holdings, Ukraine's largest privately owned oil and gas company, issued a press release announcing that Hunter Biden, the vice president's son, had been appointed to the company's board of directors. The younger Biden would "be in charge of the Holdings legal unit and provide support for the company among international organizations."[3] *Reuters* reported that the New York law firm Boies Schiller Flexner LLP, where Hunter Biden worked, would be retained by Burisma. But he was branching out. He had started an investment company called Rosemont Seneca Partners with Christopher Heinz, the stepson of former Secretary of State John

Kerry, and a deal was cut for Burisma to pay that company, too. According to John Solomon in *The Hill*, bank records show that Rosemont received "regular transfers into one of its accounts—usually more than $166,000 a month—from Burisma from spring 2014 through fall 2015, during a period when Vice President Biden was the main U.S. official dealing with Ukraine and its tense relations with Russia."[4]

Burisma's principal owner, and therefore Hunter Biden's ostensible boss, was Mykola Zlochevsky, who had served as ecology minister under the deposed president Yanukovych. When the Russia-loving Yanukovych got the boot, Zlochevsky soon found himself in a legal hot seat at the center of investigations involving his business.

Now, maybe this is all a coincidence, right?

Maybe the fact that Hunter Biden got two big paydays—for his law firm and his own firm—had *nothing* to do with being the son of the vice president of the United States, who had just been appointed to oversee relations with Ukraine and protect it from Russian hostility.

And maybe I'm the king of England!

You want to discuss bad optics? You want to discuss suspicious circumstances? You want to discuss deplorable opportunism, favoritism, and the appearance of payoffs? It all played out in public view!

Hunter Biden's Ukraine deals reek of quid pro quo influencing payments.

In fact, weeks before Biden joined the Burisma board, Britain's Serious Fraud Office had frozen $23 million of Zlochevsky's assets in a money-laundering investigation. Oliver Bullough, in his book *Moneyland: The Inside Story of the Crooks and Kleptocrats Who Rule the World*, confirms that Biden's gig was widely regarded as being tied to his father's power-broker position:

> *The White House insisted that the position was a private matter for Hunter Biden unrelated to his father's job, but that is not how anyone I spoke to in Ukraine interpreted it. Hunter Biden is an undistinguished*

*corporate lawyer with no previous Ukraine experience. Why then would
a Ukrainian tycoon hire him?"*[5]

There is no proof that Mykola Zlochevsky arranged for these deals
with a tit-for-tat understanding that Daddy Biden would come to his
rescue. But guess what? That's exactly what Joe Biden did—and he even
admitted, on video, to firing the prosecutor in charge of the investigation.

Before we get to Biden's stunning confession—something he, aston-
ishingly, bragged about—let's spend a few moments on what was going
on in corruption-crazed Ukraine with Zlochevsky, Burisma Holdings,
and Kiev prosecutors.

On February 10, 2015, Viktor Shokin was appointed prosecutor general of Ukraine. He quickly came under fire for not targeting
corruption, including in cases against former prosecutors who had
been accused of corruption. He was also lambasted abroad by the
Obama administration and other Western nations "for turning a blind
eye to corrupt practices and for defending the interests of a venal and
entrenched elite," according to the *New York Times*.[6]

Not that Shokin could have prosecuted Burisma owner Zlochevsky,
who had fled to Moscow.

Meanwhile, U.S. Ambassador Geoffrey Pyatt called the prosecutor
and Zlochevsky out in a 2015 speech:

> *For example, in the case of former Ecology Minister Mykola Zlochevsky,
> the U.K. authorities had seized 23 million dollars in illicit assets that
> belonged to the Ukrainian people. Officials at the Prosecutor General's
> office were asked by the U.K to send documents supporting the seizure.
> Instead they sent letters to Zlochevsky's attorneys attesting that there was
> no case against him. As a result, the money was freed by the U.K. court
> and shortly thereafter the money was moved to Cyprus.*[7]

But the case against Shokin is not open and shut. John Solomon,
writing for *The Hill*, contacted Shokin to talk about the case against
Zlochevsky and Burisma. He reports:

The general prosecutor's official file for the Burisma probe—shared with me by senior Ukrainian officials—shows prosecutors identified Hunter Biden, business partner Devon Archer and their firm, Rosemont Seneca, as potential recipients of money.

Shokin told me in written answers to questions that, before he was fired as general prosecutor, he had made "specific plans" for the investigation that "included interrogations and other crime-investigation procedures into all members of the executive board, including Hunter Biden."

He added: "I would like to emphasize the fact that presumption of innocence is a principle in Ukraine" and that he couldn't describe the evidence further.[8]

Shokin never got to finish that case because of—to hear Joe Biden tell it—well, Joe Biden.

On January 23, 2018, Biden appeared at a Council on Foreign Relations event. Asked about Ukraine, he began speaking about his concerns that the government there needed to address corruption. He recalled flying into Kiev for a meeting to discuss a $1 billion loan.

I was supposed to announce that there was another billion-dollar loan guarantee. And I had gotten a commitment from [then Ukraine president] Poroshenko and from [then prime minister] Yatsenyuk that they would take action against the state prosecutor. And they didn't....

I looked at them and said: I'm leaving in six hours. If the prosecutor is not fired, you're not getting the money. Well, son of a bitch. (Laughter.) He got fired. And they put in place someone who was solid at the time.[9]

Biden conveniently made no mention of his son in his 2018 speech. But Solomon reports that both U.S. and Ukrainian authorities told him that "Biden and his office clearly had to know about the general prosecutor's probe of Burisma and his son's role." These sources stressed that Hunter Biden's Ukraine gig was widely reported in American media; the U.S. embassy in Kiev, which coordinated Biden's Ukraine trip, publicly discussed the general prosecutor's case against Burisma; and "Biden's office was quoted, on the record, acknowledging Hunter Biden's role in Burisma in a *New York Times* article about the general prosecutor's Burisma case that appeared four months before Biden forced the firing of Shokin."[10]

As I write this, Joe Biden is a leading candidate to be the Democratic Party's presidential nominee in 2020. So it's no surprise that he and his son have their stories on Ukraine in sync with regard to denying this apparent self-dealing, policy-influencing-for-cash operation. Predictably, Joe Biden's campaign spokeswoman, Kate Bedingfield, says the former veep pushed to oust the former prosecutor general, Viktor Shokin, "without any regard for how it would or would not impact any business interests of his son, a private citizen." And the younger Biden claims: "At no time have I discussed with my father the company's business, or my board service, including my initial decision to join the board."[11]

But that doesn't mean Joe Biden didn't know about his son's deal—it was widely reported. So this is a ridiculous statement. The idea that Proud Papa Joe wouldn't know about his son's big score is a joke—on anyone who believes him.

As for whether or not Shokin was an ineffective prosecutor, it's almost irrelevant because Joe Biden waited until *after* his son's client got its frozen $23 million back from the U.K. to insist that Shokin get the heave-ho. So Biden was claiming to be a hero who forced the government to fire the guy who he claims wasn't prosecuting Zlochevsky. But in reality, because Biden delayed his so-called hardball act, everyone, except maybe Shokin, got their money. Zlochevsky got his $23 million; more than $3 million flowed from Ukraine to an American firm tied to Hunter Biden in 2014 and 2015, bank records show;[12] and the Ukrainian government got the billion-dollar loan.

P.S. All proceedings against Burisma Holdings and Zlochevesky were closed. In 2018, the former minister who had once fled, fearing the long arm of the law, returned to Kiev.

What a total scam!

The most disturbing thing, though, is that this is not the only instance of Hunter Biden's cashing in on his old man's prominence while Big Daddy turned a disingenuous blind eye.

Peter Schweizer's book, *Secret Empires: How the American Political Class Hides Corruption and Enriches Family and Friends*, makes a strong case that Biden piggybacked on his dad's negotiations in Beijing to broker a billion-dollar deal for Rosemont Seneca Partners—to work on behalf of America's greatest geopolitical rival: China.

Schweizer reports that in early December of 2013, Hunter Biden accompanied his father on *Air Force 2* to Asia. "For Hunter Biden, the trip coincided with a major deal that Rosemont Seneca was striking with the state-owned Bank of China," Schweizer writes. "From his perspective, the timing couldn't have been better."

While the vice president was in talks with Vice President Li Yuan-chao and separate talks with President Xi Jinping, Biden the younger was evidently fine-tuning a little business deal of his own. Writes Schweizer:

> *What was not reported was the deal that Hunter was securing. Rosemont Seneca Partners had been negotiating an exclusive deal with Chinese officials, which they signed approximately 10 days after Hunter visited China with his father. The most powerful financial institution in China, the government's Bank of China, was setting up a joint venture with Rosemont Seneca.*
>
> *The Bank of China is an enormously powerful financial institution. But the Bank of China is very different from the Bank of America.... The Bank of China is government-owned, which means that its role as a bank blurs into its role as a tool of the government. The Bank of China provides capital for "China's economic statecraft," as scholar James Reilly puts it. Bank loans and deals often occur within the context of a government goal....*
>
> *Rosemont Seneca and the Bank of China created a $1 billion investment fund called Bohai Harvest RST (BHR).... In short, the Chinese government was literally funding a business that it co-owned along with the sons of two of America's most powerful decision makers.*[13]

The only appropriate response to this is: are you kidding me?

The vice president let his son hitch a ride to China to close a billion-dollar deal with, essentially, the Chinese government, and nobody has a problem with that?

This appears to be a new form of self-dealing. It's called "son dealing," and Joe Biden is the scam's greatest proponent.

If the American people want any accountability from our leaders—and we should—Hunter Biden's profiteering off the coattails of his politically connected dad should destroy Joe Biden's presidential campaign. After all, the anti-Trump brigade just spent two years lecturing us all about the dangers of foreign collusion. Apparently, they meant only bogus collusion hoaxes involving Trump. Biden's insistence that his son is an independent businessman is beyond disingenuous. It insults the intelligence of the American electorate. It also displays utter disregard for good governance. I don't want *any* family members *anywhere* making easy-money deals because they are close to our current president or to any future president or vice president. Anyone working with the U.S. government or the administration should recognize he or she is there to perform *public service* for the good of the country, not to make family members wealthy. And I especially don't want to see a former vice president's son getting $1 billion to make investments on behalf of China—a country that aims to supplant the U.S. as a global superpower and denies its own citizens freedom of speech, religion, movement, and pretty much every other liberty you can think of. That all evidence points to Hunter Biden's profiting off his father's position is, in a word, disgusting.

In March 2019, reports appeared with evidence suggesting that the U.S. State Department and FBI pressured Ukrainian authorities to aid in the prosecution of Paul Manafort prior to the November presidential election. It was reported that Prosecutor General Yuriy Lutsenko had opened up an investigation into allegations that his country's anti-corruption wing intentionally leaked financial records—specifically the infamous "black ledger" that revealed millions of dollars in payments to Paul Manafort—in order to discredit the Trump campaign and help Hillary Clinton win the election.[14]

Lutsenko's probe was prompted by a Ukrainian parliamentarian's release of a recording purporting to quote a top law enforcement official as saying his agency leaked the Manafort financial records to help Clinton's campaign.[15]

One month later, news broke that the FBI and State Department had held a series of meetings in Washington, D.C., with Ukrainian law enforcement agents and diplomats. According to Andrii Telizhenko, a former political officer at the Ukrainian embassy, American officials asked members of the National Anti-Corruption Bureau of Ukraine (NABU) during a January 2016 meeting about locating new evidence regarding illegal payments made by Party of Regions—the pro-Russia political party of deposed president Yanukovych—and its dealings with Americans.

If this is true, it raises all kinds of questions. Manafort, at the time of this request, had not yet joined the Trump campaign and yet was seemingly back on the FBI's radar, even though the bureau had finished a 2014 investigation into Manafort without pressing any charges against the lobbyist. What would have prompted the bureau to refocus on him? Did agents know he planned to join the Trump team and, if so, how did they know?

Multiple sources within the Ukraine government confirmed the gist of Telizhenko's recollection.

> *Kostiantyn Kulyk, deputy head of the Ukraine prosecutor general's international affairs office, said that, shortly after Ukrainian authorities returned from the Washington meeting, there was a clear message about helping the Americans with the Party of the Regions case.*[16]

Manafort, as noted earlier, joined the Trump campaign in March 2016. Ukraine's NABU leaked the existence of the ledger on May 29, 2016. Coincidence? Kostiantyn Kulyk didn't sound convinced at all. "Yes, there was a lot of talking about needing help and then the ledger just appeared in public," he recalled.[17]

The handwritten ledger—which totals 400 pages and mentions Manafort's name twenty-two times—reveals that $12.7 million in undisclosed cash payments were designated for Manafort from Yanukovych's pro-Russian political party from 2007 to 2012, according to the NABU.[18]

Some of the payments were independently verified by the Associated Press, which matched at least $1.2 million in payments with bank records from Manafort's consulting firm in the U.S.[19] And while that finding confers some legitimacy on the black ledger, it still does not explain why the ledger was "discovered" only at that time.

In other words, five months after Obama administration operatives asked for help identifying Party of Regions corruption, Ukrainian investigators came out with allegedly damning evidence that pointed directly at the Trump campaign chairman. The leak seemed designed to damage the campaign's credibility along with Manafort's.

This is why I've been saying that the real conspiracy story isn't only Trump-Russia. If the black ledger was released specifically to help Clinton and hurt Trump, Mueller and the FBI spent three years investigating the wrong collusion story.

How does this fit together? Let's start with the fact that Manafort wasn't the only American political operative toiling for cash in the Ukraine. *Politico* reports that Tad Devine, a top strategist for the Al Gore 2000 and John Kerry 2004 presidential campaigns, was also working for the same guy Manafort was—Viktor Yanukovych. So was Tony Podesta! That's right! Tony, the brother of Hillary Clinton's 2016 campaign manager, John Podesta, was working with Manafort and lobbying on behalf of Yanukovych along with former Obama White House counsel Greg Craig. There were more leftist Americans, too. One of Yanukovych's rivals, incumbent president Viktor Yushchenko, had enlisted the firm run by Mark Penn, Hillary Clinton's chief strategist in her 2008 campaign.[20] Just as with Clinton, Penn's candidate failed to make it on to the final ballot, but the fact remains that there have been Democratic operatives—both consultants and diplomats—flooding Ukraine, making connections, spreading their tentacles, and scoring big paydays since Obama took over the Oval Office. Again, I thought the Democrats cared deeply about foreign "collusion"?

Tony Podesta was rumored to be under investigation for failing to register as a foreign agent, but Greg Craig has been indicted for making false statements to the Justice Department in connection with his work for Ukraine as a partner at Skadden, Arps, Slate, Meagher & Flom LLP.[21] (This is the same firm where lawyer Alex van der Zwaan worked. Zwaan copped a plea deal after Mueller's team indicted him for lying to investigators about work he had done for Manafort and his partner Rick Gates.)

Craig, who also worked in the Clinton White House, insists he is innocent of any FARA violation. There is, however, one more disturbing fact about his work in Ukraine that demonstrates how much crazy cash-based influence peddling was going on in Ukraine. Manafort steered $5.2 million to Craig in 2012, when Hillary Clinton was still secretary of state, to research and write a brief justifying the arrest of one of Yanukovych's rivals. The bulk of that payout was funded by Ukrainian oligarch Victor Pinchuk. Here's the interesting thing about Pinchuk—besides the fact that he's the fourth guy in this book named Victor/Viktor—he's a steel magnate who donated $10–25 million to the Clinton Foundation "sometime before 2013, making him the top foreign contributor to the foundation," according to one report.[22]

Let me summarize all this for you: Manafort arranged for a pal of Obama's and the Clintons' to earn a huge payday—for writing a report that glossed over political abuses of a pro-Russian president—from a billionaire who poured a record-setting amount of cash into the private foundation run by the U.S. secretary of state.[23]

In other words, Victor Pinchuk was paying to rehabilitate the reputation of the soon-to-be-booted Russia-loving president of Ukraine by forking over millions to a Democrat swamp insider *and* was showering the Clintons with cash.

Pinchuk, like an Eastern European swamp lord, seems to have been paying and playing both sides in this case—and everyone was too greedy to reject his money. And yet the only operative hit with big charges, the only guy to consistently generate front-page headlines, was Manafort. Why? Listen, there's little doubt that Manafort's personal financial activities put a target on his back—I'm not here to defend him—but he clearly wasn't the only one putting profits ahead of principle in Ukraine. Look at this list: Craig, Podesta, Penn, Devine—a supergroup of Democratic operators. Just the guys you'd want if you were looking to align with U.S. political leaders in power.

Remember, Obama was president during this entire time. Hillary Clinton was the secretary of state from 2009 to 2013. Obama and Joe Biden were, rightfully, Ukraine's protectors in 2014, when the nation bounced its Putin-pal president for refusing to strike a deal with the European Union. It's understandable, then, that in 2016 members of the Ukraine government must have felt some loyalty to Obama and Biden, who floated a billion-dollar loan to the country. If there was pressure from the Democrat-controlled swamp to produce evidence against the underdog Republican candidate who had some positive things to say about Moscow, why wouldn't the Ukrainians curry favor and reveal the black ledger they'd known about for at least two years?

"Why Manafort?" you might ask. That was the answer right there!

None of this occurred in a vacuum. As I reported in my previous book, *Spygate: The Attempted Sabotage of Donald J. Trump*, and mentioned early on in this one, a number of pro-Clinton operatives were fanning the flames when it came to Manafort, including longtime DNC employee Alexandra Chalupa, who was fixated on Manafort and his relationship with Yanukovych and fed stories to the American press. She also reportedly spent significant time at the Ukrainian embassy in Washington.

John Solomon reports that Andrii Telizhenko, the former political officer at the Ukrainian embassy, claims that senior Ukrainian diplomats instructed him to "gather whatever dirt Ukraine had in its government files about Trump and Manafort." Telizhenko says he subsequently met with Chalupa.

> She said the DNC wanted to collect evidence that Trump, his organization and Manafort were Russian assets, working to hurt the U.S. and working with [Russian president Vladimir] Putin against the U.S. interests. She indicated if we could find the evidence they would introduce it in Congress in September and try to build a case that Trump should be removed from the ballot, from the election.[24]

Meanwhile, Glenn Simpson, the man who subtly outed Paul Manafort in his 2007 *Wall Street Journal* article by noting he was not registered as a foreign lobbyist for Oleg Deripaska, was clearly monitoring the situation, at least via his employee Nellie Ohr, who testified to Congress that she had been on the lookout for "public source information" related to Manafort, Trump, and organized crime. And Ohr, as we now know, even forwarded some of her research to her husband and others at the Department of Justice.

It was about Ukraine.

And Manafort.

We've come full circle, haven't we?

We started in Ukraine—the island stopover—but we've docked back in the swamp.

I hope you can see how shrewd, manipulative political operatives and deep-pocketed players created a toxic, divisive feedback loop of distorted and fabricated negative information about Donald Trump and steered it first to the FBI and the DOJ and then to the mainstream media.

The thing about this feedback loop is that it got louder and louder until it crippled the country. It was a hideous noise composed of lies and slander, driven by politics, thirst for power, and shrewd manipulative political operatives; it fed more lies, more fear, more poison into the air. It became impossible to hear the truth.

CHAPTER 9

Fixing the Future

The U.S. Constitution is not just a piece of paper.

To me, it's the closest thing our nation has to a sacred document. And that, in many ways, is what drove me to write this book and tell this story.

If we can't agree as Democrats or Republicans, or as conservatives or liberals, on a common set of operating principles to guide the liberty-loving republic envisioned by our nation's founders and codified in our flexible but firm Constitution, we are doomed. If Russiagate makes one thing crystal clear, it's that we need to hammer out an agreement about how we use—and don't use—government intelligence resources to conduct surveillance and to spy on American citizens. We need to *clearly* define when it's appropriate. We need to establish how to conduct oversight on such usage in investigations—and how to prevent the weaponization of unconfirmed intelligence and any surveillance for political ends.

If we can't, the protection of liberty and the right to due process that are specified in the Constitution will become empty words, and the promise of America will be stripped of its future.

That would be a tragedy, not just for America but for the entire world.

As enduring as the Constitution is, its true power comes from a nation that believes in it and adheres to it. It is a flexible document—which is part of its power. But its basic truths should never be forsaken for political gain.

Russiagate should be seen as a cautionary tale for people of all political persuasions. Regardless of who the president is, Republican or Democrat, the fabrication of "raw intelligence" that was systematically laundered, fed to the FBI, and simultaneously leaked to damage and destabilize both a presidential campaign and a presidency should *never* happen again.

I don't want to beat up on FBI agents. That is not the point of *Exonerated.* I believe that 99.9 percent of bureau agents are good, upstanding patriots dedicated to enforcing the law and upholding justice. But the senior managers of the agency dropped the ball. And this was not and is not okay.

Look, this is tricky stuff. Covert cyberoperations allow bad actors to fabricate false stories. Social media offers exponential power to spread those stories. Those who know how to master the various platforms can just pour gasoline on a damaging fiction about a public figure and watch it burn down that person's career. As digital technology advances, documents can and will be falsified and doctored. Video and audio manipulation is so sophisticated that it will become difficult to ascertain whether tapes of alleged backroom deals, secret meetings, or sex acts are real or are faked *kompromat.* So the kind of intelligence manipulation at play in Russiagate is likely to grow worse. I have little doubt that counterintelligence will soon evolve from unverified written reports, like the Steele dossier, to high-tech manufactured digital "proof." God help us when bad actors sample public figures' voices and then literally put digitally faked, damaging words in their mouths.

This means our political leaders need to hatch a bipartisan set of protocols to ensure that a case like Russiagate never happens again. We need to have safeguards, and there need to be checks and balances. Where are the Democrats standing up and saying this needs to be done? Where are the Republicans who can reach out to Never Trumpers and say, "Hey, guys, look what just happened. If it happened to one president, it can happen to the next occupant in the Oval Office! We, as a nation, need to protect ourselves from this kind of grotesque abuse"?

The issues this book raises should not be viewed as political footballs and opportunities for bloviators to grandstand. National security is hugely important. But so is good governance, the right to privacy, due process, and the presumption of innocence. We need whistleblowers. They need protection. The Obama administration prosecuted more whistleblowers than all other previous administrations combined.[1] These people need to be protected, not prosecuted! History tells us that our intelligence and law enforcement agencies are not immune to abusing power. To this day, forty-seven years after his death, former FBI director J. Edgar Hoover's covert campaigns against American citizens are still being discovered. A just-published biography about Nelson Algren, the National Book Award winner for *The Man With the Golden Arm* (which was adapted into a movie starring Frank Sinatra), reveals that Hoover arranged for the leftist author's book contract to be canceled and his passport application denied in order to hurt Algren's soon-to-plummet career.[2]

I have opposed the key provisions of the PATRIOT Act for constitutional reasons, and I remain against it. America has always defined itself by protecting God-given rights and civil liberties. Law enforcement should not use unsubstantiated rumors to justify running sting operations to hurt political opponents. It should not outsource surveillance on American citizens to foreign intelligence as a way to skirt our own domestic laws. When these things happen, when politicized lawmen and government officials ignore weaponized investigations and ignore civil rights, not to mention basic fair play and decency, then we as a nation have lost our way.

Our leaders need to get back on track. They need to earn our trust. They need to figure out the best way to protect our nation from internal and external investigatory and surveillance abuses. Only when our lawmakers and law enforcers have put a system of checks and balances in place to prevent the gross exploitation we have witnessed will they, too, be exonerated.

ENDNOTES

CHAPTER 1

1 Glenn R. Simpson and Mary Jacoby, "How Lobbyists Help Ex-Soviets Woo Washington," *The Wall Street Journal*, April 17, 2007, https://www.wsj.com/articles/SB117674837248471543.

2 Ibid.

3 Ibid.

4 Matthew Continetti and Michael Goldfarb, "Fusion GPS and the Washington Free Beacon: A Note to Our Readers," *Washington Free Beacon*, October 27, 2017, https://freebeacon.com/uncategorized/fusion-gps-washington-free-beacon/.

5 Executive Session Committee on the Judiciary, and the Committee on Government Reform and Oversight, "Interview of: Bruce Ohr," August 28, 2018, https://dougcollins.house.gov/sites/dougcollins.house.gov/files/Ohr%20Interview%20Transcript%208.28.18.pdf.

6 Jack Gillum and Shawn Boburg, "'Journalism for Rent': Inside the Secretive Firm Behind the Trump Dossier," *The Washington Post*, December 11, 2017, https://www.washingtonpost.com/investigations/journalism-for-rent-inside-the-secretive-firm-behind-the-trump-dossier/2017/12/11/8d5428d4-bd89-11e7-af84-d3e2ee4b2af1_story.html?utm_term=.fb32ce0fdda4.

7 Simpson and Jacoby, "How Lobbyists Help Ex-Soviets Woo Washington."

8 Mark Hosenball, "Ex-British Spy Paid $168,000 for Trump Dossier, U.S. Firm Discloses," *Reuters*, November 1, 2017, https://www.reuters.com/article/

us-usa-trump-russia-dossier/ex-british-spy-paid-168000-for-trump-dossier-u-s-firm-discloses-idUSKBN1D15XH.

9   Lee Smith, "Did President Obama Read The 'Steele Dossier' in the White House Last August?" *Tablet*, December 20, 2017, https://www.tabletmag.com/jewish-news-and-politics/251897/obama-steele-dossier-russiagate.

10   Jeffrey H. Birnbaum and John Solomon, "Aide Helped Controversial Russian Meet McCain," *The Washington Post*, January 25, 2008, http://www.washingtonpost.com/wp-dyn/content/article/2008/01/24/AR2008012403383_pf.html.

11   Ibid.

12   Sara A. Carter, "Here's the Russian Influence Controversy that John McCain Doesn't Want You to Know About," *Circa*, June 6, 2017.

13   Kenneth P. Vogel and David Stern, "Ukrainian Efforts to Sabotage Trump Backfire," *Politico*, January 11, 2017, https://www.politico.com/story/2017/01/ukraine-sabotage-trump-backfire-233446.

14   Ibid.

15   Ibid.

16   Michael Isikoff, "Trump's Campaign Chief is Questioned About Ties to Russian Billionaire," Yahoo! News, April 26, 2016, https://www.yahoo.com/news/trumps-campaign-chief-ducks-questions-about-214020365.html.

17   Office of the Director of National Intelligence, "Assessing Russian Activities and Intentions in Recent US Elections," January 6, 2017, https://www.dni.gov/files/documents/ICA_2017_01.pdf.

18   Cristina Maza, "Vladimir Putin's Adviser Tells Americans: 'Russia Interferes In Your Brains, We Change Your Conscience,'" *Newsweek*, February 12, 2019, https://www.newsweek.com/russia-president-vladimir-putin-election-americans-1327793.

CHAPTER 2

1   John O. Brennan (@JohnBrennan), "Donald Trump's press conference performance in Helsinki rises to & exceeds the threshold of 'high crimes & misdemeanors.' It was nothing short of treasonous. Not only were Trump's comments imbecilic, he is wholly in the pocket of Putin. Republican Patriots: Where are you???" Twitter, July 16, 2018, 8:52 a.m., https://twitter.com/johnbrennan/status/1018885971104985093?lang=en.

2   Lee Smith, "How CIA Director John Brennan Targeted James Comey," *Tablet*, February 9, 2018, https://www.tabletmag.com/jewish-news-and-politics/255020/how-cia-director-john-brennan-targeted-james-comey.

3 Luke Harding, Stephanie Kirchgaessner, and Nick Hopkins, "British Spies Were First to Spot Trump Team's Links with Russia," *The Guardian*, April 13, 2017, https://www.theguardian.com/uk-news/2017/apr/13/british-spies-first-to-spot-trump-team-links-russia.

4 Paul Wood, "Trump 'Compromising' Claims: How and Why Did We Get Here?" BBC, January 12, 2017, https://www.bbc.com/news/world-us-canada-38589427.

5 Steve Benen, "CIA Warned Lawmakers about Russia's Pro-Trump Efforts Last Summer," *The Rachel Maddow Show*, April 7, 2017, http://www.msnbc.com/rachel-maddow-show/cia-warned-lawmakers-about-russias-pro-trump-efforts-last-summer.

6 Mark Mazzetti and Carl Hulse, "Inquiry by C.I.A. Affirms It Spied on Senate Panel," *The New York Times*, July 31, 2014, https://www.nytimes.com/2014/08/01/world/senate-intelligence-commitee-cia-interrogation-report.html.

7 Lee Moran, "James Clapper: Donald Trump May Be a Russian Asset 'Whether Witting or Unwitting,'" *HuffPost*, February 20, 2019, https://www.huffpost.com/entry/james-clapper-donald-trump-russian-asset_n_5c6d1b63e4b0f40774ca4015.

8 Glenn Kessler, "James Clapper's 'Least Untruthful' Statement to the Senate," *The Washington Post*, June 12, 2013, https://www.washingtonpost.com/blogs/fact-checker/post/james-clappers-least-untruthful-statement-to-the-senate/2013/06/11/e50677a8-d2d8-11e2-a73e-826d299ff459_blog.html?utm_term=.40ba0c636edd.

9 Mollie Reilly, "James Clapper: I Gave 'Least Untruthful' Answer Possible On NSA Surveillance," *Huffington Post*, June 11, 2013, https://www.huffpost.com/entry/james-clapper-nsa-surveillance_n_3424620.

10 Jonathan Easley, "GOP Report: Clapper Told CNN Host About Trump Dossier in 2017," *The Hill*, April 27, 2018, https://thehill.com/policy/national-security/385278-gop-report-clapper-told-cnn-host-about-trump-dossier-in-2017.

11 James Clapper on Anderson Cooper 360, CNN, July 18, 2018, http://www.cnn.com/TRANSCRIPTS/1807/18/acd.01.html.

12 Nathan Layne and Jonathan Landay, "Manafort Had $10 Million Loan from Russian Oligarch: Court Filing," *Reuters*, June 27, 2018, https://www.reuters.com/article/us-usa-trump-russia-manafort/manafort-had-10-million-loan-from-russian-oligarch-court-filing-idUSKBN1JN2YF.

13 Rowan Scarborough, "Hillary Clinton, Glenn Simpson Anti-Trump Conspiracy Investigation Deepens," *Associated Press*, https://www.apnews.com/e89664dca31b75d1aadb69bba3ddc39c.

14 Jeff Carlson, "Why Would Fusion GPS's Simpson Invoke the First Amendment?" *Epoch Times*, October 19, 2018, https://www.theepochtimes.com/why-is-glenn-simpson-invoking-the-first-amendment_2694938.html.

15　Christopher Steele, "The Steele Dossier" as published by *BuzzFeed* under the title "These Reports Allege Trump Has Deep Ties To Russia," January 10, 2017, https://www.buzzfeednews.com/article/kenbensinger/these-reports-allege-trump-has-deep-ties-to-russia#.xw7n2vrB

16　Mark Maremont, "Key Claims in Trump Dossier Said to Come from Head of Russian-American Business Group," *The Wall Street Journal*, January 24, 2017, https://www.wsj.com/articles/key-claims-in-trump-dossier-came-from-head-of-russian-american-business-group-source-1485253804.

17　George Papadopoulos, *Deep State Target: How I Got Caught in the Crosshairs of the Plot to Bring Down President Trump,* hardcover ed. (New York: Diversion Books, 2019), 114.

18　Ibid., 125.

19　Gillum and Boburg, "'Journalism for Rent.'"

20　"McCabe Says He Ordered the Obstruction of Justice Probe of President Trump," CBS News. February 14, 2019, https://www.cbsnews.com/news/andrew-mccabe-says-he-ordered-the-obstruction-of-justice-case-of-president-trump-60-minutes/?fbclid=IwAR2vb9zaK1Lnw_9QIFsKNSLrdI1AaDiskANBWFMS39qdB_3_1DkOQovVjog.

21　Brian Molongoski,"Stefanik Questions FBI Director Comey During Intelligence Hearing," *NNY360*, March 20, 2017, https://www.nny360.com/opinion/stefanik-questions-fbi-director-comey-during-intelligence-hearing-video/article_1b3f678f-008a-584c-84c4-67666ff489f0.html.

22　Robert Mueller and Patrick Leahy, "Written Questions of Senator Leahy to Honorable Robert Mueller III," June 6, 2002, https://fas.org/irp/agency/doj/fisa/fbi082903.pdf.

23　Chris Reeves, "DOJ Documents Show Carter Page Helped FBI Catch Russian Spies," *Townhall*, February 5, 2018, https://townhall.com/tipsheet/chrisreeves/2018/02/05/doj-documents-show-carter-page-helped-fbi-catch-russian-spies-n2444651.

24　Paul Sperry, "Exclusive: FBI Kept from U.S. Spy Court Russian View of Carter Page As 'an Idiot,'" *Real Clear Investigations*, May 5, 2018, https://www.realclearinvestigations.com/articles/2018/09/05/fbi_kept_from_fisa_court_russian_view_of_page_as_idiot.html.

25　Sperry, "FBI Hid from FISA Court Russian View Carter Page Was an 'Idiot,'" *Real Clear Investigations*, September 6, 2018, https://www.realclearpolitics.com/2018/09/06/fbi_hid_from_fisa_court_russian_view_carter_page_was_an_039idiot039_452540.html.

26　"In Re Carter W. Page, a U.S. Person," FISA Surveillance Court Orders and Applications, FBI, October, 2016, https://vault.fbi.gov/d1-release/d1-release/view.

27 Ibid., 16.

28 WSJ Editorial Board "The Flynn Entrapment," *The Wall Street Journal*, December 12, 2018, https://www.wsj.com/articles/the-flynn-entrapment-11544658915.

29 "Rosenstein on Comey Memo: 'I Wrote It. I Believe It. I Stand By It,'" Fox News, May 19, 2017, https://www.foxnews.com/politics/rosenstein-on-comey-memo-i-wrote-it-i-believe-it-i-stand-by-it.

30 Andrew G. McCabe, *The Threat: How the FBI Protects America in the Age of Terror and Trump* (New York: St. Martin's Press, 2019), 234.

31 United States Foreign Intelligence Surveillance Court, "Rules of Procedure," November 1, 2010, https://www.fisc.uscourts.gov/sites/default/files/FISC%20Rules%20of%20Procedure.pdf.

32 Rod J. Rosenstein, "Scope of Investigation and Definition of Authority," Department of Justice, August 2, 2017, https://www.documentcloud.org/documents/4429989-Rod-Rosenstein-memo-outlining-scope-of-Mueller.html.

33 Easley, "Mueller Lieutenant Sent Email Saying He Was Proud of Sally Yates," *The Hill*, December 5, 2017, https://thehill.com/homenews/administration/363422-mueller-lieutenant-sent-email-saying-he-was-proud-of-sally-yates.

CHAPTER 3

1 Austin Wright, "Nunes Claims Some Trump Transition Messages Were Intercepted," *Politico*, March 22, 2017, https://www.politico.com/story/2017/03/devin-nunes-donald-trump-surveillance-obama-236366.

2 Alain Kredo, "Former U.N. Amb. Power Unmasked 'Hundreds' in Final Year of Obama Admin," *Washington Free Beacon*, August 2, 2017, https://freebeacon.com/national-security/former-u-n-amb-power-unmasked-hundreds-last-year-obama-admin/.

3 Manu Raju, "Exclusive: Rice Told House investigators Why She Unmasked Senior Trump Officials," CNN, September 18, 2017, https://www.cnn.com/2017/.09/13/politics/susan-rice-house-investigators-unmasked-trump-officials/index.html.

4 Eric Holder, "Government's Submission of Amendments to Standard Minimization for FBI Electronic Surveillance Minimization Procedures…" Office of U.S. Attorney General, April 23, 2012, https://www.dni.gov/files/documents/0315/Motion%20for%20Amendments%20to%20Standard%20Minimization%20Procedures%20April%2023%202012.pdf.

5 Ibid.

6   Luke Rosiak, "FISA Motion Allowed FBI to Share US Citizens' Info with Foreign Agencies. Here's How That May Have Played into the Russia Probe," *The Daily Caller*, May 3, 2019, https://dailycaller.com/2019/04/03/fbi-fisa-motion-trump-russia/.

7   Papadopoulos, *Deep State Target*, 60.

8   Ibid., 76–77.

9   Ibid., 87.

10 Solomon, "What Professor Really Told FBI about Trump, Russia and Papadopoulos," *The Hill*, August 29, 2018, https://thehill.com/hilltv/rising/404275-what-professor-really-told-fbi-about-trump-russia-and-papadopoulo.

11 Harding, Kirchgaessner, and Hopkins, "British Spies Were First to Spot Trump Team's Links with Russia."

12 Dan Bongino, "The George Papadopoulos Interview You've Been Waiting For," *The Dan Bongino Show*, November 2, 2018, https://bongino.com/the-george-papadopoulos-interview-youve-been-waiting-for/.

13 T. A. Frank, "The Surreal Life of George Papadopoulos," *The Washington Post Magazine*, May 20, 2019, https://www.washingtonpost.com/news/magazine/wp/2019/05/20/feature/the-surreal-life-of-george-papadopoulos/?noredirect=on&utm_term=.a2b89c94ea0d.

14 Raphael Satter, "Malta Academic in Trump Probe Has History of Vanishing Acts," *Associated Press*, October 22, 2018, https://www.apnews.com/800354d636af47f3afbd19338a377887.

15 Ivan Pentchoukov, "Spy Operation on Trump Campaign Started as Early as December 2015, New Texts Suggest," *Epoch Times*, June 6, 2018, https://www.theepochtimes.com/spy-operation-on-trump-campaign-started-as-early-as-december-2015-new-texts-suggest_2551831.html.

16 Michael Kranz, "British Intelligence Reportedly Told the CIA Months Before the Election That Trump's Campaign Had Illicit Contacts with Russia," *Business Insider,* March 5, 2018, https://www.businessinsider.com/uk-told-cia-about-trump-russia-contacts-before-election-2018-3.

17 Brennan Interview on "Morning Joe," MSNBC, March 25, 2019.

18 Catherine Herridge and Cyd Upson, "Lisa Page Testimony: Collusion Still Unproven by Time of Mueller's Special Counsel Appointment," Fox News, September 16, 2018, https://www.foxnews.com/politics/lisa-page-testimony-collusion-still-unproven-by-time-of-muellers-special-counsel-appointment.

19 "Read FBI's Strzok, Page Texts About Trump," Fox News, January 21, 2018, https://www.foxnews.com/politics/read-fbis-strzok-page-texts-about-trump.

20 Chuck Ross, "Cambridge Academic Reflects on Interactions with 'Spygate' Figure," *The Daily Caller*, April 4, 2019, https://dailycaller.com/2019/04/04/cambridge-halper-flynn-spygate/.

21 Adam Goldman, Mazzetti, and Matthew Rosenberg, "F.B.I. Used Informant to Investigate Russia Ties to Campaign, Not to Spy, as Trump Claims," *The New York Times*, May 18, 2018, https://www.nytimes.com/2018/05/18/us/politics/trump-fbi-informant-russia-investigation.html.

22 Ibid.

23 Ross, "Cambridge Academic Reflects on Interactions With 'Spygate' Figure."

24 Laura Jarrett, "CIA, FBI, Director of National Intelligence Working with Attorney General Barr to Review Russia Probe Origins," CNN, May 14, 2019, https://www.cnn.com/2019/05/14/politics/russia-investigation-origin-barr-haspel-coats-wray/index.html.

25 Ben Riley-Smith and Robert Mendick, "Theresa May's Spy Chiefs Were Briefed on Explosive Christopher Steele Dossier Before Donald Trump," *The Telegraph*, https://www.telegraph.co.uk/news/2019/05/19/theresa-mays-spy-chiefs-briefed-explosive-chistopher-steele/.

26 Jim Sciutto,Pamela Brown, and Eric Bradner, "British Intelligence Passed Trump Associates' Communications with Russians on to US Counterparts," CNN, April 14, 2017, https://www.cnn.com/2017/04/13/politics/trump-russia-british-intelligence/index.html.

27 Rosenstein, "Order No. 3915-2017 Appointment of Special Counsel to Investigate Russian Interference With the 2016 Presidential Election and Related Matters," May 7, 2017, https://www.justice.gov/opa/press-release/file/967231/download.

CHAPTER 4

1 George Neumayr, "John Brennan's 'Exceptionally Sensitive' Issue," *The Spectator*, January 15, 2019, https://spectator.org/john-brennans-exceptionally-sensitive-issue/.

2 Sharon LaFraniere, Mazzetti, and Matt Apuzzo, "How the Russia Inquiry Began: A Campaign Aide, Drinks and Talk of Political Dirt," *The New York Times*, December 30, 2017, https://www.nytimes.com/2017/12/30/us/politics/how-fbi-russia-investigation-began-george-papadopoulos.html.

3 Eric Felten, "FBI Man's Testimony Points to Wrongdoing Well Beyond Spying," *Real Clear Investigations*, April 12, 2019, https://www.realclearinvestigations.com/articles/2019/04/11/fbi_mans_testimony_points_to_significant_wrongdoing_beyond_spying.html.

4 Ibid.

5 Nolan D. McCaskill, "Meadows: Papadopoulos' House Interview Shows Weakness of Mueller's Probe," *Politico*, October 25, 2018, https://www.politico.com/story/2018/10/25/papadopoulos-mueller-house-interview-941110.

6　Papadopoulos, *Deep State Target*, 187-188.

7　Foreign Intelligence Surveillance Act of 1978 "FISA," 50 U.S.C. § 702.

8　"In Re Carter W. Page, a U.S. person," FISA Surveillance Court Orders and Applications, FBI, October, 2016, https://vault.fbi.gov/d1-release/d1-release/view.

9　Julian Borger, "John McCain Passes Dossier Alleging Secret Trump-Russia Contacts to FBI," *The Guardian*, January 11, 2017,https://www.theguardian.com/us-news/2017/jan/10/fbi-chief-given-dossier-by-john-mccain-alleging-secret-trump-russia-contacts.

10　Ibid.

11　Clara Fitts and Scott F. Mann, "Fact Sheet: The Foreign Intelligence Surveillance Court," Center for Strategic & International Studies, February 27, 2014 https://www.csis.org/analysis/fact-sheet-foreign-intelligence-surveillance-court.

12　"Upstream vs. Prism," The Electronic Frontier Foundation, https://www.eff.org/pages/upstream-prism.

13　"Memorandum Opinion and Order," United States Foreign Intelligence Surveillance Court, April 26, 2017, https://www.dni.gov/files/documents/icotr/51117/2016_Cert_FISC_Memo_Opin_Order_Apr_2017.pdf.

14　Ibid.

15　Jeff Carlson, "The Uncovering—Mike Rogers' Investigation, Section 702 FISA Abuse & the FBI," The Markets Work, April 15, 2018, https://themarketswork.com/2018/04/05/the-uncovering-mike-rogers-investigation-section-702-fisa-abuse-the-fbi/.

16　"Intelligence Branch," The FBI, https://www.fbi.gov/about/leadership-and-structure/intelligence-branch.

17　Jerry Dunleavy, "Justice Department Worried About 'Bias' of Confidential Source in FISA Application Based on Christopher Steele Dossier," *The Washington Examiner*, March 22, 2019, https://www.washingtonexaminer.com/news/justice-department-worried-about-bias-of-confidential-source-in-fisa-application-based-on-chiristopher-steele-dossier.

18　Solomon, "Nellie Ohr's 'Hi Honey' Emails to DOJ About Russia Collusion Should Alarm Us All," *The Hill*, May 1, 2019, https://thehill.com/opinion/white-house/441580-nellie-ohrs-hi-honey-emails-to-doj-about-russia-collusion-should-alarm-us.

19　Ibid.

20　"Interview of Bruce Ohr," Committee on The Judiciary, Joint with the Committee on Government Reform and Oversight, August 28, 2018, https://dougcollins.house.gov/sites/dougcollins.house.gov/files/Ohr%20Interview%20Transcript%208.28.18.pdf

21　Ibid.

22 Steele, "The Steele Dossier."

23 Ibid.

24 Mark Tran, "WikiLeaks to publish more Hillary Clinton emails - Julian Assange," *The Guardian*, June 12, 2016, https://www.theguardian.com/media/2016/jun/12/ wikileaks-to-publish-more-hillary-clinton-emails-julian-assange.

25 Apuzzo and Maggie Haberman, "Trump Associate Boasted That Moscow Business Deal 'Will Get Donald Elected,'" *The New York Times*, August 28, 2017, https://www. nytimes.com/2017/08/28/us/politics/trump-tower-putin-felix-sater.html.

26 Steele, "The Steele Dossier."

27 Maremont, "Key Claims in Trump Dossier."

28 "In Re Carter W. Page, a U.S. Person," FISA Surveillance Court Orders and Applications, FBI, October, 2016, https://vault.fbi.gov/d1-release/d1-release/view.

29 Michael Isikoff, "U.S. Intel Officials Probe Ties Between Trump Adviser and Kremlin," Yahoo! News, September 23, 2016, https://www.yahoo.com/news/u-s-intel-officials-probe-ties-between-trump-adviser-and-kremlin-175046002.html.

30 Scarborough, "Michael Isikoff: Dossier's Trump-Russia Collusion Claims 'Likely False,'" AP News, December 30, 2018, https://www.apnews.com/ b40bb54f4bc829849daaa98624dba031.

31 "In Re Carter W. Page, a U.S. Person," FISA Surveillance Court Orders and Applications, FBI, January, 2017, https://vault.fbi.gov/d1-release/d1-release/view.

32 Ibid. January Application 2017.

33 Ibid.

34 FISA, April Application 2017.

35 Simpson and Jacoby, "How Lobbyists Help Ex-Soviets Woo Washington."

36 Carter, "Here's the Russian Influence Controversy that John McCain Doesn't Want You to Know About."

37 Simpson and Jacoby, "How Lobbyists Help Ex-Soviets Woo Washington."

38 Birnbaum and Solomon, "Aide Helped Controversial Russian Meet McCain."

39 Maza, "Here's Where Paul Manafort Did Business with Corrupt Dictators," *Newsweek*, August 7, 2018, https://www.newsweek.com/heres-where-paul-manafort-did-business-corrupt-dictators-1061470.

40 Carter, "Here's the Russian Influence Controversy that John McCain Doesn't Want You to Know About."

41 Ibid.

42 "Deposition of David Kramer," United States District Court for the Southern District of Florida, December 13, 2017, https://www.scribd.com/document/401932342/ Kramer-Depositioin#from_embed?campaign=VigLink&ad_group=xxc1xx&-source=hp_affiliate&medium=affiliate.

43 Ibid.

44 John McCain and Mark Salter, *The Restless Wave: Good Times, Just Causes, Great Fights, and Other Appreciations* (New York: Simon & Schuster, 2018), 241.

CHAPTER 5

1 Papadopoulos, *Deep State Target*, 60.
2 Ross, "Devin Nunes Casts Doubt on Joseph Mifsud Narrative in Letter to Intel Agencies," *The Daily Caller*, May 5, 2019, https://dailycaller.com/2019/05/04/Nunes-mifsud-papadopoulos/.
3 Papadopoulos, *Deep State Target*, 99.
4 Ibid.
5 Byron York, "Trump Campaign Vet: Informant Used Me to Get to Papadopoulos," *The Washington Examiner*, May 28, 2018, https://www.washingtonexaminer.com/news/trump-campaign-vet-sam-clovis-says-informant-used-him-to-get-to-papadopoulos.
6 Papadopoulos, *Deep State Target*, 101–102.
7 Goldman, Michael S. Schmidt, and Mazzetti, "F.B.I. Sent Investigator Posing as Assistant to Meet with Trump Aide in 2016," *The New York Times*, May 2, 2019, https://www.nytimes.com/2019/05/02/us/politics/fbi-government-investigator-trump.html.
8 Papadopoulos, *Deep State Target*, 106.
9 Ibid., 61.
10 Ibid., 87.
11 Select Committee on Intelligence—Republicans, "Ranking Member Nunes Demands Information on Mifsud From Government Agencies," Youtube video of a Fox News clip, 4:53, May 20, 2019, https://www.youtube.com/watch?v=-WP_FSujL4Y.
12 Easley, "GOP Report: Clapper Told CNN Host About Trump Dossier."
13 Adam Entous, Ellen Nakashima, and Philip Rucker, "Justice Department Warned White House That Flynn Could Be Vulnerable to Russian Blackmail, Officials Say," *The Washington Post*, February 13, 2017, https://www.washingtonpost.com/world/national-security/justice-department-warned-white-house-that-flynn-could-be-vulnerable-to-russian-blackmail-officials-say/2017/02/13/fc5dab88-f228-11e6-8d72-263470bf0401_story.html?utm_term=.cedf72afa7da.
14 David S. Cloud, "Yates Warned White House That Trump's National Security Advisor 'Could Be Blackmailed' by Moscow," *The Los Angeles Times*, May 8, 2017, https://www.latimes.com/nation/la-na-pol-senate-yates-testimony-20170508-story.html.

15 Robert S. Mueller III, "Report on the Investigation into Russian Interference in the 2016 Presidential Election," vol. 2, 23, https://www.nytimes.com/interactive/2019/04/18/us/politics/mueller-report-document.html#g-page-235.

16 Ibid, citing his 302 interview.

17 James B. Comey, "Statement for the Record Senate Select Committee on Intelligence," June 8, 2017, https://www.intelligence.senate.gov/sites/default/files/documents/os-jcomey-060817.pdf.

18 Apuzzo and Rosenberg, "Sessions Is Likely to Be Grilled on Reports of Meeting with Russian Envoy," *The New York Times*, June 12, 2017, https://www.nytimes.com/2017/06/12/us/politics/sessions-is-likely-to-be-grilled-on-reports-of-meeting-with-russian-envoy.html?mcubz=1.

19 Schmidt, Mazetti, and Apuzzo, "Trump Campaign Aides Had Repeated Contacts with Russian Intelligence," *The New York Times*, February 14, 2017, https://www.nytimes.com/2017/02/14/us/politics/russia-intelligence-communications-trump.html?module=inline.

20 Washington Post Staff, "Full Transcript: FBI Director James Comey Testifies on Russian Interference in 2016 Election," *The Washington Post*, March 20, 2017, https://www.washingtonpost.com/news/post-politics/wp/2017/03/20/full-transcript-fbi-director-james-comey-testifies-on-russian-interference-in-2016-election/?utm_term=.6f2e4f300a07.

CHAPTER 6

1 Comey, "James Comey's Prepared Remarks for Testimony," *The New York Times*, June 7, 2017, https://www.nytimes.com/interactive/2017/06/07/us/politics/document-Comey-Prepared-Remarks-Testimony.html.

2 Apuzzo, Haberman, and Rosenberg, "Trump Told Russians That Firing 'Nut Job' Comey Eased Pressure from Investigation," *The New York Times*, May 19, 2017, https://www.nytimes.com/2017/05/19/us/politics/trump-russia-comey.html.

3 Ibid.

4 Schmidt, "In a Private Dinner, Trump Demanded Loyalty. Comey Demurred," *The New York Times*, May 11, 2017, https://www.nytimes.com/2017/05/11/us/politics/trump-comey-firing.html.

5 Schmidt, "Comey Memo Says Trump Asked Him to End Flynn Investigation," *The New York Times*, May 16, 2017, https://www.nytimes.com/2017/05/16/us/politics/james-comey-trump-flynn-russia-investigation.html.

6 Terry Gross, "Andrew McCabe: FBI Investigations into Trump 'Were Extraordinary Steps,'" NPR, February 19, 2019, https://www.npr.org/2019/02/19/695646320/andrew-mccabe-fbi-investigations-into-trump-were-extraordinary-steps.

7   Chris Smith, "Rod Rosenstein's Revenge—And What Comes Next," *Vanity Fair*, May 18, 2017, https://www.vanityfair.com/news/2017/05/rod-rosensteins-revenge.

8   Ibid.

9   "General Powers of Special Counsel: § 600.1 - Grounds for Appointing a Special Counsel," Department of Justice, https://www.customsmobile.com/regulations/expand/title28_chapterVI_part600_section600..1.

10 "Who Monitors or Oversees the FBI?" FBI.gov, https://www.fbi.gov/about/faqs/who-monitors-or-oversees-the-fbi.

11 Ann Parks, "A Conversation with Rod J. Rosenstein U.S. Attorney for the District of Maryland," *The Daily Record*, July 14, 2005, https://thedailyrecord.com/2005/07/14/a-conversation-with-rod-j-rosenstein-us-attorney-for-the-district-of-maryland/.

12 Rosenstein, "Order No. 3915-2017."

13 Office of the Inspector General. "Report of Investigation: Recovery of Text Messages from Certain FBI Mobile Devices," *Politico*, https://www.politico.com/f/?id=00000167-a934-df8f-adff-a97d48360000.

14 Ibid.

15 Jeff Mordock and Alex Swoyer, "Three of the Five FBI Employees Dinged for Anti-Trump Bias in IG Report Ended Up on Mueller Probe," *The Washington Times*, June 20, 2018, https://www.washingtontimes.com/news/2018/jun/20/peter-strzok-lisa-page-and-kevin-clinesmith-anti-t/.

16 Mueller, "Report on the Investigation into Russian Interference," vol. 1, 183.

17 "A Top FBI Lawyer Is Allegedly Under Investigation of Leaking Classified Information to the Media," *Circa*, July 27, 2017.

18 Papadopoulos, *Deep State Target*, 158–163.

19 Carol D. Leonnig, Tom Hamburger, and Rosalind S. Helderman, "FBI Conducted Raid of Former Trump Campaign Chairman Manafort's Home," *The Washington Post*, August 9, 2017, https://www.washingtonpost.com/politics/fbi-conducted-pre-dawn-raid-of-former-trump-campaign-chairman-manaforts-home/2017/08/09/5879fa9c-7c45-11e7-9d08-b79f191668ed_story.html?utm_term=.da3e5d6d5f0e.

20 Ibid.

21 Financial Crimes Enforcement Network, "Report of International Transportation of Currency or Monetary Instruments," Department of the Treasury, https://fincen.gov/sites/default/files/shared/fin105_cmir.pdf.

22 Papadopoulos, *Deep State Target*, 170.

23 Ibid., 133.

24 Ibid.

25 Rosenstein, "Scope of Investigation."

26 Mueller, "Report on the Investigation into Russian Interference," vol. 1, 11.

27 Jefferson B. Sessions III, "Letter of Resignation," Office of the Attorney General, http://apps.washingtonpost.com/g/documents/world/read-jeff-sessions-letter-of-resignation/3298/.

28 Quinta Jurecic, "Document: Indictment of Roger Stone," *Lawfare*, January 25, 2019, https://www.lawfareblog.com/document-indictment-roger-stone.

CHAPTER 7

1   Politico Staff, "Full Text: James Comey Testimony Transcript on Trump and Russia," *Politico*, June 8, 2017, https://www.politico.com/story/2017/06/08/full-text-james-comey-trump-russia-testimony-239295.

2   Ibid.

3   Ibid.

4   Mueller, "Report on the Investigation into Russian Interference," vol. 2, 73.

5   Tim Hains, "President Trump's Full Interview with Lester Holt: Firing of James Comey," *Real Clear Politics*, May 11, 2017, https://www.realclearpolitics.com/video/2017/05/11/president_trumps_full_interview_with_lester_holt.html.

6   18 U.S.C. § 1512, https://www.law.cornell.edu/uscode/text/18/1512.

7   Will Chamberlain, "Checkmate. How President Trump's legal team outfoxed Mueller," *Human Events*, May 1, 2019, https://humanevents.com/2019/05/01/checkmate/.

8   Sadie Gurman and Aruna Viswanatha, "Trump's Attorney General Pick Criticized an Aspect of Mueller Probe in Memo to Justice Department," *The Wall Street Journal*, December 20, 2018, https://www.wsj.com/articles/trumps-attorney-general-pick-criticized-an-aspect-of-mueller-probe-in-memo-to-justice-department-11545275973.

9   Ibid.

10 William Barr to Rosenstein and Steve Engel, memorandum, "Mueller's 'Obstruction Theory,'" https://int.nyt.com/data/documenthelper/549-june-2018-barr-memo-to-doj-mue/b4c05e39318dd2d136b3/optimized/full.pdf#page=.

11 Ibid.

12 Ibid.

13 Mueller, "Report on the Investigation into Russian Interference," vol. 1, 6–7.

14 Mueller, "Report on the Investigation into Russian Interference," vol. 2, 156–157.

15 "Read Attorney General William Barr's Summary of the Mueller Report," *The New York Times*, March 24, 2019, https://www.nytimes.com/interactive/2019/03/24/us/politics/barr-letter-mueller-report.html.

16 Ibid.

17 Matthew Kahn, "Document: Robert Mueller's Letter to Bill Barr," *Lawfare*, March 27, 2019, https://www.lawfareblog.com/document-robert-muellers-letter-bill-barr.

18 Gaslighting is a popular term for a psychological tactic that occurs when a person tries to achieve power over a victim by denying the victim's reality. The phrase is based on the classic 1944 movie *Gaslight* (and the 1938 play it was adapted from). In the silver screen suspense-drama, Charles Boyer plays an abusive husband who tries to make his wife, played by Ingrid Bergman, feel as if she's gone mad.

19 Kimberly A. Strassel, "The Russians and the Dossier," *The Wall Street Journal*, April 25, 2019, https://www.wsj.com/articles/the-russians-and-the-dossier-11556232721.

20 Ibid.

21 Matthew Kahn, "Document: Robert Mueller's Letter to Bill Barr," *Lawfare*, March 27, 2019, https://www.lawfareblog.com/document-robert-muellers-letter-bill-barr.

22 Rosenstein, "Order No. 3915-2017."

23 Mueller, "Report on the Investigation into Russian Interference," vol. 2, 182.

24 Mueller, "Report on the Investigation into Russian Interference," vol. 2, 8.

25 Ibid.

26 Ibid.

27 Rosenstein, "Order No. 3915-2017."

28 Papadopoulos, *Deep State Target*, 60.

29 Mueller, "Report on the Investigation into Russian Interference," vol. 1, 83.

30 John Sweeney and Innes Bowen, "Joseph Mifsud: The Mystery Professor Behind Trump Russia Inquiry," BBC, March 21, 2018, https://www.bbc.com/news/world-us-canada-43488581.

31 Lee Smith, "The Maltese Phantom of Russiagate," *RealClear Investigations*, May 30, 2018, https://www.realclearinvestigations.com/articles/2018/05/26/the_maltese_phantom_of_russiagate_.html

32 Andrew McCarthy, "The FBI's Trump-Russia Investigation Was Formally Opened on False Pretenses," *The National Review*, May 6, 2019, https://www.nationalreview.com/2019/05/fbi-trump-russia-investigation-george-papadopoulos.

33 Mueller, "Report on the Investigation into Russian Interference," vol. 1, 193.

34 Ibid., 94.

35 Paul Sperry (@paulsperry_), "Funny how Mueller cites numerous email exchanges Papadopoulos had in 2016 in the footnotes of his report, yet he cites not a single one of Papadopoulos' emails with one 'Azra Turk.' Hmm. Wonder why. Another example of how Mueller's probe was really designed to protect the FBI/DOJ," Twitter, May 2, 2019, 2:29 p.m., https://twitter.com/paulsperry_/status/1124063293017075712.

36 Kathleen Kavalec, "Kavalec Memo," U.S. Department of State, October 11, 2016, https://www.scribd.com/document/409364009/Kavalec-Less-Redacted-Memo.

37 Ibid.

38 Ibid.

39 Kavalec, "State Department Handwritten Notes of Meeting with Christopher," U.S. Department of State, https://www.scribd.com/document/409363897/State-Department-handwritten-notes-of-meeting-with-Christopher-Steele.

40 Ross, "Steele Identified Russian Dossier Sources, Notes Reveal," *The Daily Caller*, May 16, 2019, https://dailycaller.com/2019/05/16/steele-dossier-sources-state-department.

41 Charles Grassley and Ron Johnson "Letter to William Barr," April 25, 2019, https://www.grassley.senate.gov/sites/default/files/documents/2019-04-25%20CEG%20RJ%20to%20DOJ%20%28Surveillance%20of%20Trump%20Transition%20Team%29.pdf.

42 Ibid.

43 "Read the Emails on Donald Trump Jr.'s Russia Meeting," *The New York Times*, July 11, 2017, https://www.nytimes.com/interactive/2017/07/11/us/politics/donald-trump-jr-email-text.html.

44 Mueller, "Report on the Investigation into Russian Interference," vol 1, 185.

45 "Interview of Glenn Simpson," Senate Judiciary Committee, 77, August 27, 2017. https://www.documentcloud.org/documents/4345511-Sen-Judiciary-interview-with-Glenn-Simpson.html.

46 "Interview of Rinat Akhmetshin," Senate Judiciary Committee, November 14, 2017, https://www.judiciary.senate.gov/imo/media/doc/Akhmetshin%20Transcript_redacted.pdf.

47 Mueller, Vol. 2, 23.

48 Erica Orden et al., "Michael Cohen Pleads Guilty, Says He Lied About Trump's Knowledge of Moscow Project," CNN, November 29, 2018, https://www.cnn.com/2018/11/29/politics/michael-cohen-guilty-plea-misleading-congress/index.html.

49 Mueller, "Report on the Investigation into Russian Interference," vol. 2, 139.

50 Ibid.

51 Ibid., 153.

52 Ibid., 155.

53 Mueller, "Report on the Investigation into Russian Interference," vol. 1, 5.

54 Congressman Matt Gaetz, "Gaetz Appears on 'The Story' with Martha MacCallum to Discuss the Mueller Report," Youtube video, 4:18, April 22, 2019, https://www.youtube.com/watch?v=i8OA4Zizruw.

55 Mueller, "Report on the Investigation into Russian Interference," Vol 1, 198.

56 "Read Attorney General William Barr's Summary of the Mueller Report," *The New York Times*, March 24, 2019, https://www.nytimes.com/interactive/2019/03/24/us/politics/barr-letter-mueller-report.html.

57 Ibid.

CHAPTER 8

1   Fox News, "Transcript: Rep. Maloney: Trump Has Been Appalling in His Conduct Regardless of Legality," April 18, 2019, https://www.foxnews.com/transcript/rep-maloney-trump-has-been-appalling-in-his-conduct-regardless-of-legality.

2   Kenneth P. Vogel and Iuliia Mendel, "Biden Faces Conflict of Interest Questions that Are Being Promoted by Trump and Allies," *The New York Times*, May 1, 2019, https://www.nytimes.com/2019/05/01/us/politics/biden-son-ukraine.html.

3   Burisma Holdings, "Hunter Biden Joins the Team of Burisma Holdings," press release, May 12, 2014, https://www.documentcloud.org/documents/5980032-Burisma-Announces-Hunter-Biden-s-Appointment-to.html.

4   Solomon, "Joe Biden's 2020 Ukrainian Nightmare: A closed Probe Is Revived," *The Hill*, April 1, 2019, https://thehill.com/opinion/white-house/436816-joe-bidens-2020-ukrainian-nightmare-a-closed-probe-is-revived.

5   Oliver Bullough, *Moneyland: The Inside Story of the Crooks and Kleptocrats Who Rule the World* (New York: St. Martin's Press, 2019), 114.

6   Andrew E. Kramer, "Ukraine Ousts Viktor Shokin, Top Prosecutor, and Political Stability Hangs In Balance," *The New York Times*, March 29, 2016, https://www.nytimes.com/2016/03/30/world/europe/political-stability-in-the-balance-as-ukraine-ousts-top-prosecutor.html.

7   U.S. Embassy Kyiv Ukraine, "Remarks by US Ambassador Geoffrey Pyatt at the Odesa Financial Forum on September 24, 2015," Facebook post, September 24, 2015, https://www.facebook.com/usdos.ukraine/posts/10153248488506936

8   Solomon, "Joe Biden's 2020 Ukrainian Nightmare."

9   Richard N. Haass, "Foreign Affairs Issue Launch with Former Vice President Joe Biden," Council on Foreign Relations, January 23, 2018, https://www.cfr.org/event/foreign-affairs-issue-launch-former-vice-president-joe-biden.

10 Solomon, "Joe Biden's 2020 Ukrainian Nightmare."

11 Kenneth P. Vogel and Iuliia Mendel, "Biden Faces Conflict of Interest Questions That Are Being Promoted by Trump and Allies," *The New York Times*, May 1, 2019, https://www.nytimes.com/2019/05/01/us/politics/biden-son-ukraine.html?smid=nytcore-ios-share.

12 Solomon, "Joe Biden's 2020 Ukrainian Nightmare."

13 Peter Schweizer, *Secret Empires: How the American Political Class Hides Corruption and Enriches Family and Friends* (New York: Harper, 2018), 36–41.

14 Solomon, "As Russia Collusion Fades, Ukrainian Plot to Help Clinton Emerges," *The Hill*, March 20, 2019, https://thehill.com/opinion/campaign/435029-as-russia-collusion-fades-ukrainian-plot-to-help-clinton-emerges.

15 Ibid.

16 Solomon, "How the Obama White House Engaged Ukraine to Give Russia Collusion Narrative an Early Boost," April 25, 2019, https://thehill.com/opinion/white-house/440730-how-the-obama-white-house-engaged-ukraine-to-give-russia-collusion.

17 Ibid.

18 Kramer, Andrew E. et al. "Secret Ledger in Ukraine Lists Cash for Donald Trump's Campaign Chief." *The New York Times*. Aug. 14, 2016. https://www.nytimes.com/2016/08/15/us/politics/paul-manafort-ukraine-donald-trump.html

19 Gillum, Chad Day, and Jeff Horwitz, "AP Exclusive: Manafort Firm Received Ukraine Ledger Payout," April 12, 2017, https://www.apnews.com/20cfc75c82eb4a67b94e624e97207e23.

20 Ben Smith and Vogel, "Obama Consultants Land Abroad," *Politico*, November 18, 2009, https://www.politico.com/story/2009/11/obama-consultants-land-abroad-029410.

21 Vogel and Katie Benner, "Gregory Craig, Ex-Obama Aide, Is Indicted on Charges of Lying to Justice Dept," *The New York Times*, April 11, 2019, https://www.nytimes.com/2019/04/11/us/politics/gregory-craig-indictment.html.

22 Ivan Pentchoukov, "Clinton Foundation Donor Funded Ukraine Report at Core of Charges Against Former Obama Counsel," *The Epoch Times*, April 16, 2019, https://www.theepochtimes.com/clinton-foundation-donor-funded-ukraine-report-at-core-of-charges-against-former-obama-counsel_2881961.html.

23 Ibid.

24 Solomon, "Ukrainian Embassy Confirms DNC Contractor Solicited Trump Dirt in 2016," *The Hill*, May 2, 2019, https://thehill.com/opinion/white-house/441892-ukrainian-embassy-confirms-dnc-contractor-solicited-trump-dirt-in-2016.

CHAPTER 9

1 Spencer Ackerman and Ed Pilkington, "Obama's War on Whistleblowers Leaves Administration Insiders Unscathed," *The Guardian*, March 16, 2015, https://www.theguardian.com/us-news/2015/mar/16/whistleblowers-double-standard-obama-david-petraeus-chelsea-manning.

2   Jonathan Dees, "Nelson Algren's Street Cred," *The New Yorker*, April 8, 2019, https://
     www.newyorker.com/magazine/2019/04/15/nelson-algrens-street-cred.

ABOUT THE AUTHOR

Dan Bongino is a former Secret Service agent, NYPD Police Officer, and a former Republican nominee for the U.S. Senate and the House. He is a multiple-time *New York Times* bestselling author and he is the host of the top-ranked podcast *The Dan Bongino Show.*